COLLEGE STUDY

The Essential Ingredients

SECOND EDITION

SALLY A. LIPSKY

INDIANA UNIVERSITY OF PENNSYLVANIA

PEARSON

Prentice
Hall

Upper Saddle River, New Jersey
Columbus, Ohio

Library of Congress Cataloging-in-Publication Data

Lipsky, Sally.
   College study : the essential ingredients / Sally A. Lipsky. — 2nd ed.
      p. cm.
Includes bibliographical references and index.
ISBN-13: 978-0-13-158524-9 (pbk.)
ISBN-10: 0-13-158524-X (pbk.)
1. Study skills.   2. Critical thinking—Study and teaching (Higher)   I. Title.
LB2395.L49 2008
378.1'0281—dc22

2007002105

Vice President and Executive Publisher: Jeffery W. Johnston
Executive Editor: Sande Johnson
Editorial Assistant: Lynda Cramer
Production Editor: Alexandrina Benedicto Wolf
Production Coordination: Thistle Hill Publishing Services, LLC
Design Coordinator: Diane C. Lorenzo
Cover Design: Jason Moore
Cover Image: Jupiter Images
Production Manager: Susan Hannahs
Director of Marketing: David Gesell
Marketing Manager: Amy Judd
Marketing Coordinator: Brian Mounts

This book was set in Janson Text by Integra Software Services. It was printed and bound by
R.R. Donnelley & Sons Company. The cover was printed by Phoenix Color Corp.

Pearson Education Ltd.
Pearson Education Singapore Pte. Ltd.
Pearson Education Canada, Ltd.
Pearson Education–Japan

Pearson Education Australia Pty. Limited
Pearson Education North Asia Ltd.
Pearson Educación de Mexico, S.A. de C.V.
Pearson Education Malaysia Pte. Ltd.

10 9 8 7 6 5 4 3 2 1
ISBN-13: 978-0-13-158524-9
ISBN-10:   0-13-158524-X

In loving memory of Irene and Merle

BRIEF CONTENTS

CHAPTER 1	CHAPTER 2	CHAPTER 3	CHAPTER 4	CHAPTER 5	CHAPTER 6	CHAPTER 7	CHAPTER 8
Academic Success	Managing Time	Study Environment	Active Listening	Reading Textbooks	Enhancing Memory	Test Success	Continuing Success

CONTENTS

Chapter 3

CONTROLLING YOUR STUDY ENVIRONMENT   38

Chapter 4

ACTIVE LISTENING AND NOTE TAKING   49

Chapter 5

READING AND STUDYING TEXTBOOKS   75

Chapter 6

ENHANCING YOUR MEMORY   100

Chapter 7

SUCCESS WITH TESTS   111

Chapter 8

CONTINUING YOUR ACADEMIC SUCCESS: A REVIEW   143

REFERENCES   147

INDEX   148

Note: Every effort has been made to provide accurate and current Internet information in this book. However, the Internet and information on it are constantly changing, so it is inevitable that some of the Internet addresses listed in this textbook will change.

CHAPTER 1	CHAPTER 2	CHAPTER 3	CHAPTER 4	CHAPTER 5	CHAPTER 6	CHAPTER 7	CHAPTER 8
Academic Success	Managing Time	Study Environment	Active Listening	Reading Textbooks	Enhancing Memory	Test Success	Continuing Success

PREFACE

The text contains a complete and balanced coverage of essential learning and study techniques, with an emphasis on critical thinking at the college level. Readers are exposed to *how* to learn, while understanding *why* they learn, within the context of making informed choices about strategies that work best for them. After immediate transfer of a specific learning strategy into daily academic life, students critique its effectiveness. Content is organized to help students become self-regulating learners and problem solvers.

Features

The text integrates three separate yet interrelated elements of how students learn:

1. *Strategies:* Covers important and practical study techniques that students can apply immediately in their daily academic courses.
2. *Attitude:* Provides opportunities for students to explore their levels of interest, motivation, and commitment toward transferring learning techniques in their day-to-day lives as college students.
3. *Learning styles:* Individual differences in learning preferences and tendencies can be a contributing factor in the successful implementation of learning and study strategies. As such, readers become aware of and apply techniques that match *how they learn best.*

New: The VARK Questionnaire—an instrument assessing *visual, aural, read/write, and kinesthetic* preferences for learning—is incorporated within the text.

Additional features of the text include the following:

Critical Thinking Task

- **New:** Additional strategies for *online learning.*
- **New:** Activities involving *critical, creative, or problem-solving thinking skills,* designated by the corresponding icon. Examples are analyzing academic behaviors and attitudes, critiquing why a strategy does or does not work, predicting

and solving academic problems, differentiating types of test questions, and creating or modifying study aids that match an individual's learning style.

- **New:** *Comprehension checks* at the end of each chapter allow students to check their understanding and recall of key content.
- **New:** The *Companion Website* (www.prenhall.com/lipsky) contains supplemental activities for readers, problem-solving scenarios centered on topics presented in the text, added learning style information and activities, PowerPoint™ presentations for class instruction, a course-culminating assignment from Chapter 8, and sample lesson plans for each chapter. Also included are templates for typing responses to text activities, including *Pause . . . and Reflect*, *Personal Action Statement*, and *Assess Your Success* exercises. This icon indicates that an exercise is on the Companion Website.
- Streamlined format and an informal, personal writing style maintain *reader's attention*.
- Focus on *modeling* the essentials of learning helps readers apply strategies to course work. Illustrations of how peers apply specific strategies, in the form of visual examples and students' comments, provide both appealing and convincing models.
- Relevant activities immediately *engage* readers.

This text is intended for use in either a two-year or four-year institution within a variety of contexts:

- A study skills or learning strategies course
- A skills course linked or paired with content-area course work
- An introductory-level content course using a supplemental learning strategies text
- A first-year orientation program or seminar
- A series of workshops for first-year students or students on academic probation
- A peer educator training course requiring a college learning strategies text

To the Student: An Introduction to Text Features

AT THE BEGINNING OF CHAPTERS

- **Focus questions.** Examine the focus questions when previewing the chapter. Then read to discover the answers to the questions. This strategy will help you become a more perceptive and involved reader.
- **Chapter terms.** Review these key concepts before reading the chapter. When you have completed the chapter, check your understanding by providing both a meaning and an example for each term.

WITHIN CHAPTERS

- **Pause . . . and Reflect.** These exercises provide opportunities to think about and process key ideas. Questions will guide your observations and commentary. Your instructor may ask you to share your reflections as part of a group discussion or activity.
- **Models.** Use these illustrative examples of how other college students applied strategies in a variety of courses as templates for your own course work.
- **Student voices.** Interspersed within chapters are compelling comments from other college students. Reading about your peers' experiences and suggestions can help guide and motivate you to apply similar strategies.
- **Try it out!** These exercises direct you to *apply* immediately a strategy introduced in the chapter, a crucial aspect of developing a personal system of study.
- **Assess Your Success.** After trying out a strategy, evaluate your performance by answering a series of questions.

Critical
Thinking
Task

- **Critical Thinking Tasks.** The corresponding icon indicates that a particular section or activity involves critical, creative, or problem-solving thinking skills.

AT THE END OF CHAPTERS

- **Personal Action Statements** are specific strategies you will choose to implement within a designated time frame. After implementing your Personal Action Statements, you will *Assess Your Success* with the purpose of identifying what techniques do and do not work for you. Through this process—choosing, using, and assessing strategies—you will work toward building an effective and efficient study system for yourself.
- **Chapter summaries** provide a practical overview of the essential strategies and are a useful reference for future semesters.
- **Comprehension checks** remind you to go back to the first page of each chapter and answer the focus questions and define the chapter terms.

For the Instructor

An Instructor's Manual accompanies the text and includes these features:

- **New:** Information and activities linking text chapters with two widely used instruments:

    The Myers-Briggs Type Indicator (MBTI) personality inventory, a standardized instrument for assessing personality types or preferences (Briggs & Myers, 1998).

    The Learning and Study Strategies Inventory (LASSI), a self-report instrument assessing college students' use of and attitudes toward learning and study strategies (Weinstein & Palmer, 2002).

New: Pages for *overhead transparencies.*

Suggestions on how to use text features for in-class activities, including small-group collaborative work, journal writing, and group discussion.

Five-point *chapter quizzes* provide a modest check of students' comprehension. Instructors may choose to use the quizzes as an extrinsic incentive for students to read assigned chapters.

A *sample syllabus,* including an outline of activities for a one-credit or two-credit college learning skills course.

Acknowledgments

We would like to thank the following reviewers for their constructive comments to improve this book: Sarah Bedingfield, New Hampshire Community Technical College; Dolores Bryznicki, Indiana University of Pennsylvania; Christina Chapman, Lewis and Clark Community College; Arden Hamer, Indiana University of Pennsylvania; Judith Pula, Frostburg State University; Barbara Sherman, Liberty University; Kim Smokowski, Bergen Community College; Elizabeth Stewart, City College of San Francisco; and Cathy Stephenson, Indiana University of Pennsylvania.

CHAPTER 1

Creating Academic Success

FOCUS QUESTIONS

What are the three essential ingredients of a system of study?

Why is each important?

How am I going to apply each?

CHAPTER TERMS

After reading this chapter, define (in your own words) and provide an example for each of the following terms:

- active learning behaviors
- extrinsic reward
- intrinsic reward
- learning style
- passive learning behaviors
- Personal Action Statement

1

A System of Study: The Essential Ingredients

As a college student, you no doubt have experienced—or will experience— approaches toward instruction and requirements for learning unlike your previous years of education. Recent high school graduates often welcome the greater personal and social freedoms associated with college life. However, along with these freedoms come challenges. No longer does a teacher or a parent oversee your learning; at the postsecondary level, you, the student, are expected to be a self-directed and self-motivated learner.

For the nontraditional student, college life offers a different set of challenges: Returning to school after a hiatus often creates a complicated juggling act among job, family, and academic responsibilities. Whatever the personal circumstances, individual students require their own set of learning strategies to meet the multifaceted challenges encountered at the college level effectively. This text provides you, the student, with the tools for developing these strategies so that you become a self-directed learner and are able to achieve academic success throughout your college career.

By the time you enter college, you have developed a system of study based on three essential ingredients:

1. Your learning behaviors
2. Your learning attitudes
3. Your learning style

Each of these is discussed in the following sections.

Your Learning Behaviors

The term *learning behaviors* refer to a variety of actions done in an academic situation. These learning behaviors combine to form your system of study. Note that some behaviors are conducive to learning, such as arriving at class several minutes early with notepaper and pen, sitting in the front and middle of a classroom, listening attentively and selectively, asking questions to clarify points, reviewing notes after class, seeking out help when needed, and so on. These are termed **active learning behaviors** because they represent self-responsibility, initiative, and involvement in the learning process. Active learning behaviors lead to successful outcomes—that is, high grades and a smooth path toward graduation.

In contrast, a host of behaviors impede learning, such as skipping classes, sleeping during class, yielding to distractions, studying after social and leisure activities, and not seeking assistance. These are termed **passive learning behaviors.** Students exhibiting these behaviors do *not* take charge of their learning. Passive learners often are not accustomed to working hard in school; they tend to devote minimal time and effort in their academic life.

This text will introduce you to active learning behaviors at the college level. Each chapter focuses on a group of active learning behaviors—or strategies—related to a major study skills topic. Principal elements of each topic are labeled "Essential Ingredients." Within each chapter you will be given choices of which behaviors, or strategies, you will put into practice as you engage in your day-to-day college course work.

Your Learning Attitudes

our attitude toward all aspects of academic life (going to class, interacting with the instructors, completing assignments, studying) has a huge impact on your accomplishments in college. Successful college students exhibit the following characteristics:

- **Motivation.** They *want* to achieve and are determined to reach their academic goals.
- **Persistence.** They do not let hurdles block personal achievement. When problems arise, they seek out help and persevere until a satisfactory solution is reached.
- **Self-Discipline.** They are willing to make the necessary sacrifices and devote the necessary efforts to receive that college degree.
- **A Personal Support Network.** They have at least one family member or close friend they can rely on for personal encouragement and support. Likewise, they tend to associate with peers who are responsible and caring.

How many of these characteristics do you exhibit at this point in your college career? As you read the upcoming chapters in this text, you will be exploring your outlook toward the many aspects of college life and determining if your attitudes work *for* or *against* your immediate and long-term successes.

A note about online courses: Because distance education can be a very anonymous and independent process, your level of motivation, persistence, and self-discipline are especially important. Oftentimes students enroll in online courses for reasons that work *against* their success. For example, they are disinterested in the subject, want to get the course out of the way, or think distance education courses are easier than face-to-face instruction. You are much more likely to do well in online course work if you assume the mind-set of "What can I learn?" as opposed to "How little can I do to pass?"

Keep in mind that in college, *you* will be determining your own academic path; thus it is up to you to take responsibility for your successes—or failures. This mission of self-determination and responsibility can be accomplished by an awareness of *why* you are here, *what* you want to accomplish, and *how* you can develop a viewpoint that contributes to personal success.

Critical Thinking Task

pause... *and reflect*

- What motivates *you* to achieve?
- Are you persistent when faced with a problem or stumbling block? Provide a personal example.
- Research indicates that self-discipline is more important than I.Q. in predicting academic success. Why do you think this is? Would you describe yourself as self-disciplined in regard to school? In what areas are you self-disciplined? Describe in what areas you are not self-disciplined, and explain why.
- Who is part of your personal support network?

Your Learning Style

Your learning behaviors and attitudes are, to some degree, shaped by what is termed your **learning style,** which refers to preferences in behaviors characteristic of each person, that is, *how a person learns best.* For instance, one student prefers to discuss new course information with others, and she takes advantage of weekly study groups. Another student prefers to study alone in a quiet location allowing him to create detailed flow charts summarizing the new information. Both students are just as effective with their studying, yet both follow differing paths in *how* they study. This is part of their individual preferences, or learning style, that they have developed throughout the years. By assessing and analyzing your learning style, you can create a system of study that is both comfortable and successful for you.

ASSESSING YOUR LEARNING STYLE

A widely used method to define learning style is by a person's preference for sensory modes of learning. The VARK questionnaire is an informal instrument that assesses how individuals prefer to take in or receive and give out or express information via *visual, aural, read/write,* and *kinesthetic* modalities. Each of these modalities are explained after you complete the VARK.

try it out!

Complete either the hard-copy version here (see Figure 1.1), or for the online version at www.vark-learn.com/english/index/asp, go to Questionnaire.

The VARK. FIGURE **1.1**

Directions: For each item, choose the answer that best explains your preference and circle the letter(s) next to it. **Circle more than one** if a single answer does not match your perception. Leave blank any question that does not apply.

1. You are helping someone who wants to go to your airport, business district, or bus station. You would:
   a) draw or give her a map.
   b) tell her the directions.
   c) write down the directions (without a map).
   d) go with her.

2. You are not sure whether a word should be spelled dependent or dependant. You would:
   a) see the word in your mind and choose by the way they look.
   b) think about how each word sounds and choose one.
   c) find it in a dictionary.
   d) write both words on paper and choose one.

3. You are planning a trip for a group. You want some feedback from them about the plan. You would:
   a) use a map or Website to show them the places.
   b) phone, text-message, or e-mail them.
   c) give them a copy of the printed itinerary.
   d) describe some of the highlights.

4. You are going to cook something as a special treat for your family. You would:
   a) look through the cookbook for ideas from the pictures.
   b) ask friends for suggestions.
   c) use a cookbook in which you know there is a good recipe.
   d) cook something you know without the need for instructions.

5. A group of tourists want to learn about the parks in your area. You would:
   a) show them pictures on the Internet, photographs, or picture books.
   b) talk about or arrange a talk for them about parks.

(continued)

FIGURE   **1.1**   *Continued.*

    c) give them a book or pamphlets about the parks.

    d) take them to a park and walk with them.

6. You are about to purchase a digital camera or cell phone. Other than price, what would most influence your decision?

    a) A modern design and looks good.

    b) Salesperson telling me about its features.

    c) Reading the details about its features.

    d) Trying or testing it.

7. Recall a time when you learned how to do something new. Try to avoid choosing a physical skill, such as riding a bike. You learned best by:

    a) diagrams and charts (visual clues).

    b) listening to somebody explaining it and asking questions.

    c) written instructions, such as a manual or textbook.

    d) watching a demonstration.

8. You have a problem with your knee. You would prefer that the doctor:

    a) showed you a diagram of what was wrong.

    b) described what was wrong.

    c) gave you a Web address or something to read about it.

    d) used a plastic model of a knee to show what was wrong.

9. You want to learn a new program, skill, or game on a computer. You would:

    a) follow the diagrams in the book that came with it.

    b) talk with people who know about the program.

    c) read the written instructions that came with the program.

    d) use the controls or keyboard.

10. I like Websites that have:

    a) interesting design and visual features.

    b) audio channels where I can hear music, radio programs, or interviews.

    c) interesting written descriptions, lists, and explanations.

    d) things I can click on, shift, or try.

11. Other than price, what would most influence your decision to buy a new nonfiction book?

    a) The way it looks is appealing.

    b) A friend talks about it and recommends it.

Continued.   FIGURE   1.1

    c) You quickly read parts of it.

    d) It has real-life stories, experiences, and examples.

12. You are using a book, CD, or Website to learn how to take photos with your new digital camera. You would like to have:

    a) diagrams showing the camera and what each part does.

    b) a chance to ask questions and talk about the camera and its features.

    c) clear written instructions with lists and bullet points about what to do.

    d) many examples of good and poor photos and how to improve them.

13. Do you prefer a teacher or a presenter who uses:

    a) diagrams, charts, or graphs?

    b) question and answer, talk, group discussion, or guest speakers?

    c) handouts, books, or readings?

    d) demonstrations, models, or practical sessions?

14. You have finished a competition or test and would like some feedback. You would like to have feedback:

    a) using graphs showing what you had achieved.

    b) using a person who talks it through with you.

    c) using a written description of your results.

    d) using examples from what you have done.

15. You are going to choose food at a restaurant or café. You would:

    a) look at what others are eating or look at pictures of each dish.

    b) ask the server or friends to recommend choices.

    c) choose from the descriptions in the menu.

    d) choose something you have had there before.

16. You have to make an important speech at a conference or special occasion. You would:

    a) make diagrams or get graphs to help explain things.

    b) write a few key words and practice saying your speech over and over.

    c) write out your speech and learn from reading it over several times.

    d) gather many examples and stories to make the talk real and practical.

Scoring:

1. Count your choices for each letter. Write each total on the lines below.

   Total number of a's circled = _____ Visual
   Total number of b's circled = _____ Aural
   Total number of c's circled = _____ Read/write
   Total number of d's circled = _____ Kinesthetic

2. Calculate the differences between your highest score and the remaining scores.

   → If differences are 4 or more, your highest score represents your *single learning preference*.
   → If differences are 3 or less, you have a *multimodal learning preference*; that is, you have two or more dominant learning modalities.

Here are two examples:

1. Total number of a's circled = <u>8</u> Visual [5-point difference]
   Total number of b's circled = <u>3</u> Aural [10-point difference]
   Total number of c's circled = <u>7</u> Read/write [6-point difference]
   Total number of d's circled = <u>13</u> Kinesthetic [highest score]
   The highest score is 13. Subtract the other scores from 13. All of the differences are 4 or more. Thus the student's *single learning preference* is "kinesthetic."

2. Total number of a's circled = <u>9</u> Visual [highest score]
   Total number of b's circled = <u>3</u> Aural [6-point difference]
   Total number of c's circled = <u>7</u> Read/write [2-point difference]
   Total number of d's circled = <u>6</u> Kinesthetic [3-point difference]

The highest score is 9. Subtract the other scores from 9. Some of the differences are 3 or less. Thus the student has a *multimodal learning preference* with visual, read/write, and kinesthetic as the dominant modalities.

The purpose of this scoring method is for you to recognize your dominant mode(s) of learning, which can range from mild to very strong. Be aware that you likely use all four modalities at various times and in varying situations. Also, because this is an inexact scoring technique, use it as a *guideline* for identifying your favored mode(s) for learning.

Indicate your learning preference:

○ My single learning preference is (circle one) visual–aural–read/write – kinesthetic.

   or

○ My learning preference is multimodal. My dominant modalities are (circle all that apply) visual – aural – read/write – kinesthetic.

Applying/Interpreting Your Results

Keep in mind that no one mode is superior to others. You can be successful with any combination of preferences, as described next.

- **Visual learners** rely on spatial images when learning—that is, they learn best when they can see information in their mind. Visual learners often are proficient at identifying relationships among objects and ideas. When learning information, they prefer illustrations, charts, maps, and other graphic formats, including the use of color and design.

- **Aural learners** learn best when they hear information; thus they tend to prefer listening, verbalizing, and discussing new knowledge. When learning information, some aural learners favor listening to tapes or CDs, or talking aloud to themselves and others.

- **Read/write learners** prefer learning by reading—texts, handouts, directions, manuals—and by writing—lists, notes, answers to exams. They often rely on rereading and rewriting new information, organizing ideas into statements, and summarizing or turning illustrations into words. Most of your college course work will incorporate read/write modes of learning, such as reading texts, writing notes and papers, and taking essay and multiple-choice exams.

- **Kinesthetic learners** prefer to learn by doing. In learning situations, they rely on sensory feelings and prefer physical hands-on activities, such as manipulating objects, moving about, dramatizing, and going to labs or on field trips. Kinesthetic learners favor videos, photographs, and other medium with real-life scenarios. Additionally, their learning is often enhanced with the use of analogies, case studies, examples, and simulations. However, be mindful that nearly *all* students, even those with visual, auditory, or read/write preferences, benefit from application and practice of what they are learning.

- **Multimodal learners** tend to be more flexible and better able to adapt to various learning contexts. Multimodal learners tend to prefer variety and often use more than one modality and multiple strategies when learning information. Between 50% and 70% of people are considered multimodal learners.

At the end of text chapters, you will be directed to identify, implement, and evaluate specific learning and study strategies that match your learning preference as defined by visual, aural, read/write, and kinesthetic modalities. If you are multimodal, you will have even more choices of strategies to try out.

pause... *and reflect*

What are the characteristics of your learning style? Describe *how you learn best* in each of these situations:

- You are reading a novel for English.
- You are writing the first draft of a research paper.
- You are completing math homework problems.
- You are studying for a test in a science course.

As you transfer suggested learning strategies to your daily course work, you will continually assess the success or failure of the strategies. The following section describes a process to assist you with applying and assessing strategies as you build and strengthen an effective system of study throughout your college career.

A Path to Success: Personal Action Statements

A successful system of study requires much trial and error; you must *try* a strategy to know whether it will work for you. Your academic path in college will be strewn with both successes and failures. Savvy students are alert to what strategies do and do not work for them and, when needed, they take the initiative to substitute other techniques. A **Personal Action Statement** is one way to oversee the piece-by-piece construction of your overall system of study. It is a concise, step-by-step, written plan of one specific strategy—either a behavior or an attitude—that you commit yourself to do within a predetermined span of time.

Effective Personal Action Statements entail reflection, decision making, and judgment on your part. Because you are required to deliberate, analyze, and critique, each Personal Action Statement is designated as a critical thinking task within the chapters.

Use these guidelines to ensure a successful Personal Action Statement:

- Recognize that a Personal Action Statement is a *commitment to yourself* for action.
- Make the Personal Action Statement manageable by identifying a *specific step* to implement.
- Be realistic and honest with yourself. Identify a step, or strategy, that you *intend* to do, as well as hurdles and rewards for yourself.
- Be willing to put both *thought* and *time* into the Personal Action Statement. Know that, for most students, the results are worth the effort. Soon, you will become adept at identifying and outlining strategies and steps. You

will be able to see how the Personal Action Statements can *motivate* you toward action and achievement as you continue to build a system of study for yourself.

- Type your answers for each step. Writing space is limited on text pages. Furthermore, when you type you are able to make more revisions, resulting in higher quality responses. With this in mind, each Personal Action Statement and accompanying Assess Your Success are located on the companion Website where you can access templates for typing your answers.

Here is the setup for the Personal Action Statement:

1. I will: _____.
2. My greatest hurdle to achieving this is:_____.
3. I will eliminate this hurdle by: _____.
4. My time frame for achieving this is: _____.
5. My reward for achieving this is: _____.

On line 1, write what you intend to do. Write a strategy that is specific, realistic, and meaningful to you. Here are some examples:

- "I will study in a library study room three nights next week."
- "I will improve my concentration by taking short breaks every 30 minutes when reading my biology textbook."

Line 2 refers to what you anticipate as being the greatest barrier toward completing the Personal Action Statement. Relying on past experiences and your personal weaknesses, what tends to hinder successful completion of your schoolwork? Examples of hurdles are boredom, the temptation to turn on your computer games, friends dropping by to chat, and your dislike of the subject matter or the instructor. Be honest with yourself: What tends to obstruct your study plans?

On line 3, write *how* you will overcome the hurdle identified in line 2. What can you do realistically to reduce, if not eliminate, this barrier? For instance, you can study with a classmate to relieve boredom, or leave your computer games at home, or be more assertive with your friends, or talk to your professor about your problems.

On line 4, indicate your time frame. When are you going to implement this Personal Action Statement? Make the time frame immediate; begin as soon as possible.

On line 5, identify a reward for completing your Personal Action Statement successfully. It can be an **intrinsic reward** (such as a sense of satisfaction with a high test grade or increased confidence from knowing subject matter) or an **extrinsic reward** (such as watching a favorite television program, talking on the phone to a friend, or buying an ice cream cone).

After completing the Personal Action Statement, place it in an accessible location (such as above your desk, in your planner, or on your desktop computer screen) so that you can refer to it regularly to remind yourself about your intentions.

The last, yet very important, step in this process is the follow-up. At the conclusion of implementing your Personal Action Statement, assess critically what happened. Did you accomplish all that you set out to accomplish? If so, great—reward yourself! Think about the factors that contributed to your success. Use the follow-up as a time to evaluate what happened and anticipate building on your successes.

Also, learn from your partial successes as well as failures. If everything did not work out as anticipated, do not berate yourself. Keep in mind that risk taking is an inherent part of change, and it is inevitable that you will not always be successful when taking risks. However, do learn from your ineffective Personal Action Statements. Analyze what happened. Often students make their Personal Action Statements either too general or too unrealistic (refer to the examples that follow). Think about how you can shape your Personal Action Statement to make it more specific and/or practical.

TOO GENERAL:	**MORE SPECIFIC:**
I will improve my time management.	I will write class assignments in my planner.
TOO UNREALISTIC:	**MORE REALISTIC:**
I will study in the library for three hours *every night* this week.	I will study in the library for two hours on three days this week.

How about the anticipated hurdle? Did it actually emerge? If so, were you able to overcome it effectively? Did you discover other impediments? Furthermore, was your time frame appropriate for completing the Personal Action Statement?

Finally, examine your reward. Did you identify a reward that is meaningful to you? Your reward should motivate you to finish a task and make you feel good about succeeding. Dangle a reward in front of yourself that you really want— and can have!

Answering these and similar questions will aid you in analyzing what learning strategies do and do not work for you. It takes deliberate practice to develop effective Personal Action Statements, but the practice is worthwhile. Not only will you be learning about valuable college study strategies, but you also will be learning about yourself!

Conclusion

 our success in college depends on a combination of factors: your behaviors in and out of class, your attitude and commitment to working hard, your awareness of key learning strategies, and your commitment to apply and assess these strategies in your daily life. The following checklist contains keys to a successful academic year, elements that directly relate to success, satisfaction, and, ultimately, graduation from college. As the year progresses, review the checklist periodically with the goal of accomplishing as much as you can to keep yourself on the track of academic success.

KEYS TO A SUCCESSFUL ACADEMIC YEAR

1. **Be aware of *why* you are attending college, as well as what you expect to get out of college.** Whose decision was it to attend college, yours or your parents? Are you attending the college of your choice? Do you intend to graduate from this or from another college? What do you expect to accomplish in college? Be honest with yourself and clear in your goals.

2. **Know what is *expected of you* in each subject.** Read each syllabus. Make an appointment with each instructor. Attend all classes. Go to review sessions or form your own study group. Ask, and then write down the answers!

3. **Manage your time *wisely*.** Establish a routine; be aware of the dangers of too much free and unstructured time. Muster the self-discipline to say no to tempting people and activities. Also, create a balance among your academic, personal, and social/leisure lives. Assess your priorities periodically: Do you typically place your academic responsibilities *before* your social aspirations? Do you allow yourself time for fun between the academic and personal demands on your time?

4. **Develop and *use* effective methods of study.** Create a study system that is advantageous to you; choose, use, and evaluate recommended learning strategies. Form beneficial habits early in the year.

5. ***Involve yourself* in college life.** Students who participate in academic, social, and personal campus activities tend to do better academically. Create a link between yourself and other people within the college community. Make commitments like these:
   - Join a student organization or club related to your interests or major.
   - Obtain a campus job.
   - Participate in academic support services, such as tutoring, group study sessions, and workshops, or become a tutor or peer educator.
   - Go to campus cultural events, such as guest speakers, fine arts productions, and museum exhibits.
   - Participate in intramural sports and other extracurricular activities.

6. ***Avoid* these hazards:**
   - Mishandling of your personal freedom and time
   - Misuse of alcohol and drugs
   - Mishandling of your personal health
   - Mishandling of your best interests

pause... *and reflect*

Refer to the checklist that offered keys to a successful academic year. As a starting point in your college career, where would you place yourself?

For each of the six items, write a short paragraph assessing yourself at this point. Include what you have done as well as what you still need to accomplish.

try it out!

Create a sample Personal Action Statement by choosing one of the items that you still need to accomplish for a successful academic year. Use the following examples as models.

Critical
Thinking
Task

EXAMPLES OF PERSONAL ACTION STATEMENTS

1. I will: *become more involved in campus life by obtaining an on-campus job.*
2. My greatest hurdle to achieving this is: *not knowing where campus jobs are advertised.*
3. I will eliminate this hurdle by: *(1) asking my adviser about job listings during our meeting on Wednesday, and (2) inquiring at the career services office.*
4. My time frame for completing this is: *by Thursday of this week.*
5. My reward for achieving this is: *the self-satisfaction of knowing that I began looking for a job early in the semester!*

1. I will: *set aside definite times during the afternoon to do both math and chemistry problems.*
2. My greatest hurdle to achieving this is: *the distractions of TV and my computer in my apartment.*
3. I will eliminate this hurdle by: *studying at a solitary desk at the library during the afternoons when I have large chunks of free time.*
4. My time frame for completing this is: *next Tuesday.*
5. My reward for achieving this is: *not having unfinished work hanging over my head.*

1. I will: *join a campus club related to my interest in an outdoor sport.*
2. My greatest hurdle to achieving this is: *not knowing what clubs are here.*
3. I will eliminate this hurdle by: *checking the Website for the Office of Student Organizations and narrowing my options to two or three clubs that I will contact and visit.*

4. My time frame for completing this is: *within the next 2 weeks.*
5. My reward for achieving this is: *the knowledge that I actually followed through with something, as well as looking forward to meeting other students.*

Your Personal Action Statement

1. I will: _____
_____
_____

2. My greatest hurdle to achieving this is: _____
_____
_____

3. I will eliminate this hurdle by: _____
_____
_____

4. My time frame for achieving this is: _____
_____
_____

5. My reward for achieving this is: _____
_____
_____

Comprehension Check

eturn to page 1. Without looking back through the chapter, provide a complete answer for each focus question. Then, define each chapter term in your own words and provide an example.

C H A P T E R 2

Managing Your Time

FOCUS QUESTIONS

How effectively do I manage my time each day?

Why do college students often have difficulties with managing their time productively?

What are five essential strategies for successful time management?

CHAPTER TERMS

After reading this chapter, define (in your own words) and provide an example for each of the following terms:

- academic planner
- procrastination
- self-regulating attitudes and behaviors
- weekly block schedule

ESSENTIAL INGREDIENTS

College Studying

Controlling Your Time: Five Essential Ingredients

Many college students face the challenge of how to manage their daily use of time effectively. As a college student, you likely are—or soon will be—juggling a variety of responsibilities and tasks, both personal and academic. The freedom you experience as an undergraduate college student often is unparalleled. For the first time, you are making many daily decisions without having a parent or teacher oversee you. For instance, you decide what time to awaken, whether to eat breakfast, whether to attend class or start an assignment, who to socialize with, and so on. Your decisions, and the subsequent consequences of these decisions, will determine if you are successful in college or not. Read what one freshman wrote; his comments are typical of many first-time college students:

"Time management is my biggest problem. When I have to choose between leisure time and study time, leisure time always wins. I end up cramming the night before a test. One of my roommates, however, starts studying a week ahead of time for his exams and does much better than I. My problem is that nobody is here to make me study. In high school my parents made me study; here at college there always is something else I'd rather be doing." **—DEVON**

STUDENT VOICES

pause... *and reflect*

Are you similar to Devon when making daily choices and decisions about academics and studying? Answer the following questions:

1. Do you have, or anticipate having, problems choosing study time over leisure time? Describe a situation when you should have studied but did not. Why didn't you study? What did you do instead? How could you have reacted differently? What might help you choose study over leisure?

2. Do you need someone to make you study? If so, who can help you monitor your study time—a roommate, friend, tutor, or relative? Think of ways you can develop the needed self-discipline and structure to focus on academics.

3. Some college students already possess **self-regulating attitudes and behaviors** and are able to monitor their independent time consistently. Self-regulating students have developed the internal discipline, focus, and skills necessary to channel both their time and energies productively. If you fall into this category, describe how you approach your study time. What strategies and attitudes do you adopt to focus on and complete projects, assignments, and other tasks?

4. Interview a present or former student whom you consider skillful about managing his or her time. What strategies does the student use? How did he or she develop those strategies? What suggestions can the student give you about having a productive yet balanced semester? Why would you describe this student as self-regulating?

Each of the following five strategies is essential to the development of a successful system of study. As you read, consider how to incorporate each strategy into your day-to-day activities. Be aware of the importance of these strategies in reducing stress in your daily life:

1. Use a weekly block schedule.
2. Use a daily planner.
3. Use a semester calendar.
4. Balance academic with social and personal demands.
5. Avoid procrastination.

USE A WEEKLY BLOCK SCHEDULE

At the start of each semester you will be faced with many new and unfamiliar situations—different classes, instructors, on-campus or off-campus jobs, and sometimes even changes in your daily living arrangement. With these unfamiliar situations come unaccustomed expectations and responsibilities. Your most immediate need will be a schedule that provides an *overview* of what and where you should be for the week. The weekly schedule will be one tool for you to use to structure your time as you develop sound habits and routines at the beginning of each semester.

Develop a weekly routine that includes these considerations:

1. Class attendance and course work as your main priority.
2. Regular slots for study throughout the week. Look for chunks of time during the day and evening when you are the freshest.
3. Time *before* classes to refresh yourself about the day's topics.
4. Time *after* classes to go over lecture notes, work on assignments, and complete readings.

5. Ready access to a study location with minimal distractions.
6. Time to take advantage of campus support services, such as the tutorial center, writing center, counseling center, and career services.
7. Time to attend extracurricular activities, such as fine arts productions, lectures and presentations, student organizations, and community service projects.
8. Time for personal commitments, such as a job, sports, or family responsibilities.

An added personal bonus that results from following these guidelines is that you are associating with others who are responsible, successful, and have similar values and interests. As a result, you will be creating a valuable social network for yourself.

"I consider how difficult the class is for me and judge how much studying I will need. Studying earlier in the day helps me concentrate better because I am not tired. Also, I reduce my study time because I am reviewing after class when my recall is the greatest. I concentrate better during short spurts; therefore, I take advantage of the time between classes and small periods throughout the day." —RICARDO

"Using a weekly schedule has greatly reduced my procrastination (my biggest problem). I have begun utilizing those odd hours that I used to watch TV and visit friends. I now study when I feel the freshest. Also, I have become more regular in my evening study time. I find myself getting more done during the day and evening—a major difference." —JAMAL

The **weekly block schedule** (Figure 2.1) provides a visual representation of your week. By filling in the blocks you build a picture of your typical week. Follow these steps when creating a weekly schedule:

1. First, write in activities that you must do at *fixed times,* such as classes and labs, employment, commuting times, established meetings or appointments, certain family responsibilities, and practice for athletics, band, and so forth. Can you think of other established activities for your typical week?
2. Next, fill in those events for which you can establish your own times to work on and complete. Include three types of activities: academic (homework, study, tutoring); personal (meals, sleep, household tasks, errands); and social and leisure (calls/e-mails, exercise, down time).

FIGURE **2.1**   *Block format for a weekly schedule.*

MONDAY	TUESDAY	WEDNESDAY	THURSDAY	FRIDAY	SATURDAY	SUNDAY
7:00	7:00	7:00	7:00	7:00	7:00	7:00
8:00	8:00	8:00	8:00	8:00	8:00	8:00
9:00	9:00	9:00	9:00	9:00	9:00	9:00
10:00	10:00	10:00	10:00	10:00	10:00	10:00
11:00	11:00	11:00	11:00	11:00	11:00	11:00
noon	noon	noon	noon	noon	noon	noon
1:00	1:00	1:00	1:00	1:00	1:00	1:00
2:00	2:00	2:00	2:00	2:00	2:00	2:00
3:00	3:00	3:00	3:00	3:00	3:00	3:00
4:00	4:00	4:00	4:00	4:00	4:00	4:00
5:00	5:00	5:00	5:00	5:00	5:00	5:00
6:00	6:00	6:00	6:00	6:00	6:00	6:00
7:00	7:00	7:00	7:00	7:00	7:00	7:00
8:00	8:00	8:00	8:00	8:00	8:00	8:00
9:00	9:00	9:00	9:00	9:00	9:00	9:00
10:00	10:00	10:00	10:00	10:00	10:00	10:00
11:00	11:00	11:00	11:00	11:00	11:00	11:00
midnight	midnight	midnight	midnight	midnight	midnight	midnight

For *academic* time, take into account these factors:

- Schedule study time when you are most alert, using chunks of time that you have available throughout the day.
- Spread out study and review through the week, including weekends.
- Be generous with the amount of time you anticipate needing each week for out-of-class course work. When you underestimate time needed for academics, you create added complications and stress for yourself. Therefore, allow for substantial study and review time for *each course*.

Figure 2.2 shows two students' weekly block schedules. Note the differences between the two. Although each student approached the schedule with differing amounts of information and detail, both evaluated their schedules as effective for them. Note these two features of student B's schedule:

- The darkened blocks represent weekly activities established at fixed times.
- The outlined blocks represent times devoted to academic activities outside of class, including reviewing class notes, studying, and tutoring. Student B actually color-coded these outlined blocks according to subject.

Critical Thinking Task

pause.... *and reflect*

Some students (such as Student B) are more productive when they fill in nearly all of the blocks in their weekly schedule. They favor the structure of prearranged specific daily activities, including meals, sleep, study for *each* subject, and even breaks. Others (such as Student A) find this technique too restrictive and prefer to fill in only those blocks representing the most important activities.

- How about you? Are you more similar to Student A or Student B? Explain.
- Are you more productive when you plan details ahead of time or when you leave blocks open for spontaneous decisions and changes?
- What type of schedule are you more likely to follow and why?
- What type of activities should you be writing down in your weekly block schedule?
- How does time management, scheduling, and planning affect *your* levels of stress? Describe a situation in which you created stress for yourself by not managing your time adequately.

FIGURE **2.2** *Two examples of weekly block schedules.*

Student A

MONDAY	TUESDAY	WEDNESDAY	THURSDAY	FRIDAY	SATURDAY	SUNDAY
9:00 *class*	9:00	9:00 *class*	9:00	9:00 *class*	9:00	9:00
10:00 *class*	10:00 *class*	10:00 *class*	10:00 *class*	10:00 *class*	10:00	10:00
11:00 *class*	11:00	11:00 *class*	11:00 *class*	11:00	11:00	11:00
noon	noon	noon	noon	noon	noon	noon
1:00 *class*	1:00 *lab*	1:00 *class*	1:00 *lab*	1:00 *class*	1:00	1:00
2:00 *work*	2:00	2:00 *work*	2:00	2:00 *work*	2:00	2:00 *work*
3:00	3:00	3:00	3:00	3:00	3:00	3:00
4:00	4:00	4:00	4:00	4:00	4:00	4:00
5:00	5:00	5:00	5:00	5:00	5:00	5:00
6:00	6:00 *S.I. for Biol*	6:00	6:00 *S.I. for Biol*	6:00	6:00	6:00
7:00 *study*	7:00	7:00	7:00	7:00	7:00	7:00
8:00	8:00 *study*	8:00 *study*	8:00 *study*	8:00	8:00	8:00 *study*
9:00	9:00	9:00	9:00	9:00	9:00	9:00

(continued)

Continued.

FIGURE **2.2**

Student B

MONDAY	TUESDAY	WEDNESDAY	THURSDAY	FRIDAY	SATURDAY	SUNDAY
8:00	8:00 *breakfast*	8:00	8:00 *breakfast*	8:00	8:00	8:00
9:00 *breakfast*	9:00 *review for Chem*	9:00 *breakfast*	9:00 *review for Chem*	9:00 *breakfast*	9:00	9:00
10:00 *English class*	10:00 *Chem class*	10:00 *English class*	10:00 *Chem class*	10:00 *English class*	10:00 *workout*	10:00
11:00	11:00 *lunch*	11:00 *laundry*	11:00	11:00	11:00 *get ready*	11:00 *church*
noon *lunch*	noon *Chem lab*	noon *lunch*	noon *lunch*	noon *lunch*	noon *begin job*	noon *brunch*
1:00 *History class*	1:00	1:00 *History class*	1:00 *Writing Center*	1:00 *History class*	1:00	1:00
2:00 *Theater class*	2:00	2:00 *Theater class*	2:00	2:00 *Theater class*	2:00	2:00 *pack*
3:00 *review notes*	3:00 *Health class*	3:00 *review notes*	3:00 *Health class*	3:00 *pack*	3:00	3:00 *drive school*
4:00	4:00	4:00 . *Big Broth's/Sis*	4:00	4:00 *travel home*	4:00	4:00
5:00 *workout*	5:00 *dinner*	5:00 *workout*	5:00 *dinner*	5:00	5:00 *dinner*	5:00 *dinner*
6:00 *dinner*	6:00	6:00 *dinner*	6:00	6:00 *dinner*	6:00 *get ready to*	6:00
7:00 *Study Group*	7:00 *review notes*	7:00 *Chem tutoring*	7:00 *read history*	7:00	7:00 *go out*	7:00 *English 3*
8:00 *for Chem*	8:00 *Economics club*	8:00 *break*	8:00 *TV break*	8:00 *get ready to*	8:00	8:00 *history 3*
9:00 *TV break*	9:00	9:00 *study Health*	9:00 *study theater*	9:00 *go out*	9:00	9:00 *theater*
10:00 *study Health*	10:00 *prepare for class*	10:00 *floor meeting*	10:00 *finish English*	10:00	10:00	10:00 *Homework*
11:00 *SLEEP*	11:00 *SLEEP*	11:00 *SLEEP*	11:00 *SLEEP*	11:00	11:00	11:00 *SLEEP*

"By making a weekly schedule I realized how many demands there are on my time. The schedule helps me complete my work and still have time for family and leisure. Last semester I was *always* rushing to get things done. This semester I am making better judgments about my time, which is reducing the stress in my life. I could not survive without a schedule and would recommend a schedule to *every student*, especially those students juggling many responsibilities." —**NORA**

"A weekly schedule helps me see what is due for the week and figure what needs to be studied each day. Also, each night I make a schedule of classes, work, errands, and homework that I need to do the following day. And I get such a feeling of accomplishment crossing off the things that I've finished!" —**BRAD**

try it out!

1. Develop a weekly block schedule for yourself for the current semester (use Figure 2.1). Refer to the two steps described previously:
   - Fill in activities with fixed times.
   - Then fill in activities with flexible times.
2. Refer to the guidelines on pages 18–19. Consider each of the eight items when setting up your schedule.
3. After filling in your weekly block schedule, *use* it. Place it in a location for ready referral, such as over your desk, beside your calendar, near your computer screen, or in your book bag or planner. This weekly schedule will provide you with a framework for establishing your day-to-day routine, so refer to it often, especially at the start of each semester.
4. After a week, **Assess Your Success** by answering these questions:
   - Overall, did the schedule provide you with a needed framework for establishing your daily routine? Explain.
   - Should you have more or fewer activities and details in your schedule?
   - Should you use another format, different design, or color coding for your schedule?
   - Did you refer to your schedule regularly? Why or why not?
   - Will you continue to use a weekly schedule? Why or why not?

Critical Thinking Task

USE A DAILY PLANNER

An **academic planner** is a day-to-day log, either in book or electronic format, reminding you of tasks to be accomplished. It is crucial to planning and juggling schoolwork successfully with personal and social activities. A well-used planner is invaluable for keeping you on track with your many and varied plans and responsibilities. Acquire a planner that easily fits in your book bag, backpack, or purse. Carry it with you and use it daily to write down reminders.

FOR THE DAY

Jot down and prioritize what you plan to do, including

- *Academic* responsibilities for each course.
- *Personal* commitments or tasks, such as shopping, visiting a relative, or going to the bank.
- *Social* plans, such as a call home or a date with friends.

FOR THE WEEK

- Examine each course syllabus for *upcoming* lecture topics, readings, assignments, and test dates.
- Note *extracurricular* activities, such as meetings, athletic obligations, and noncredit classes.
- Be aware of *special commitments*, such as a doctor's appointment, meeting with your adviser, a tutorial appointment, a theatrical production, or a birthday celebration.

FOR THE SEMESTER

Identify key academic dates, including

- Deadline for add/drop of courses.
- Deadline for course withdrawal.
- Midterm period.
- Final exam days and times.
- Due dates for long-term course projects or papers.
- Course registration for next term.
- Breaks.

USE A SEMESTER CALENDAR

A calendar provides a long-term overview of your academic year. Use a calendar for a broad view of each semester. When you fill in important semester dates on a calendar, you create a visual picture of upcoming months, although with considerably less detail than your weekly block schedule.

Use a calendar in a similar, although less specific, manner as a planner: As suggested for your planner, chart key academic dates and assignments, projects, and

FIGURE **2.3**   *A student's calendar for November.*

SUN	MON	TUES	WED	THURS	FRI	SAT
*register for spring term this week	1	2	3	4	5	6 Melissa is visiting
6 Melissa	7 Math test Chap. 7-9	8	9	10	11 spring work application due	12 march in Veterans Way parade
13	14	15	16	17 Intr. Religion Term Paper Due	18 Accounting Test #3	19 Begin break!!
20 →	21 →	22 → Dentist app't. 1:00 pm	23 →	24 → Thanksgiving	25 →	26 →
27 travel to school	28 classes resume	29 Geography Group Presentation	30			

papers as well as special social occasions (such as someone's birthday or a friend's wedding) and personal events (such as the deadline for filing taxes or a vacation). Place the calendar in a visible location for daily reference—near your computer, over your desk, or on the kitchen bulletin board. Or use the electronic calendar in your cell phone, personal digital assistant (PDA), or computer. Publishers often place calendars within academic planners; note whether your planner provides monthly calendars that are large enough for you to write in and use.

Figure 2.3 reproduces a student's calendar for November.

try it out!

If you don't already have a planner and a calendar, get them now!

1. Fill in the planner by referring to the lists (in the previous section) of what to write down "for the day," "for the week," and "for the semester." Check off each item as you mark the information in your planner. Continue using the planner, carrying it with you throughout the day.

2. Fill in the calendar with those major events that you want to track throughout the year. Place it in a location for easy reference.

3. **Assess Your Success**: Did you use your planner daily—that is, did you write in activities and refer to it consistently? How about your calendar? Did it help you to write down major events and due dates? What is the most useful aspect of your time management system thus far? What changes will you make to build a more effective and efficient time management system?

> "Time management is a critical priority to studying, but I didn't realize it until this year. Previously I lacked the self-discipline to follow a schedule and didn't think it would be useful. *Now* I realize how much it can help! I bought a huge desk calendar to write in all my major assignments, tests, quizzes, and readings that are due throughout the term. Not only do I now have more free time, but I actually have a better attitude toward studying!" —JENNIE

STUDENT VOICES

BALANCE ACADEMIC WITH SOCIAL AND PERSONAL DEMANDS

College students often experience a conflict between their academic requirements and social desires. It is in students' best academic interest to go to sleep before midnight. However, social activities often do not happen until late at night or even in the early morning hours. In both dormitories and off-campus complexes, late-night social activities are abundant and appealing. Friends will call or stop by to chat, watch TV, play music or video games, accompany you to a party, or ask you to go to an off-campus restaurant or bar. These late-night social activities are tempting and alluring to the college student who wants relief from academic demands, as well as the chance to build a social network and personal sense of belonging.

However, over time, late-night socializing results in students who:

- Become severely sleep deprived.
- Miss classes.
- Are in a dazed, passive mode when they do attend classes.
- Do not put in quality study time during the day (instead, they are sleeping!).
- Have problems organizing, understanding, and remembering subject matter.

All of the characteristics just listed contribute to lower academic performances. Thus beware: Late-night socializing and partying can become a potent and dangerous habit!

Some students, however, especially those who are of nontraditional ages, have personal demands that can supersede their academic demands. Time tending to family responsibilities, particularly children, and employment hours can easily push aside academic requirements.

The following strategies can create a balance between your academic and social/personal desires and demands and, as a result, reduce your day-to-day stress levels:

1. *Prioritize.* Make a daily list of tasks according to an order of importance.
2. *Write down what to accomplish and when to accomplish it*, and then display your list for family and friends to see.
3. *Make others*—friends, family, and employers—*aware of your needs* and *time constraints* and ask for their *cooperation.*
4. Don't let feelings of guilt guide you in an unproductive direction. Instead, *transform feelings of guilt* into *productive* and *useful behaviors* related to attaining success in your course work.
5. *Don't overcommit yourself.* Down time is a necessity, not a luxury.
6. *Get adequate sleep.* Research studies demonstrate the drastic and negative effect of inadequate sleep on performance, concentration, and memory. Moreover, a cumulative loss of sleep is associated with increased anxiety, overeating, and illness. Establishing and maintaining a regular weekly schedule helps you get the recommended 8 to 10 hours of nightly sleep. In addition, you can improve the quality of your nighttime sleep by reducing or eliminating evening consumption of caffeine and alcohol, as well as including some form of physical activity or exercise during the day. Also, consider supplementing nighttime sleep with midday naps of no more than 60 minutes.
7. *Combine academic and social activities.* Find, or create, an environment that provides you with both solid academic activity and enjoyable social connections. Examples are study groups, tutorial or writing center services, campus organizations (such as a biology club or commuter student organization), or other groups that require study hours (such as a fraternity, sorority, or athletic team). For example, Devon (see the nearby "Student Voices") partially solved his time management problems by such a tactic.

STUDENT VOICES

"A help to me this semester, believe it or not, is pledging a fraternity. We have study sessions every Monday through Thursday from 6 to 8 P.M. in the library. This helps me, especially because the sessions are mandatory. If I don't go, I get into trouble. I have to hand in all my test grades to the scholastic chairman; if I don't get a 2.0, they won't let me in. This makes me want to do my best and is an added incentive." —DEVON

itical inking ask

pause.... *and reflect*

1. Do you have problems balancing academic demands with personal responsibilities and/or social events? Explain.
2. When faced with a choice between doing class work and taking care of personal obligations or social desires, what do you usually do? Why?
3. Is it difficult for you to say no to other people's requests, demands, or temptations? Why?
4. Follow these steps:
   - Identify your primary academic obligations for this week.
   - Next, identify your current personal responsibilities.
   - Identify your current social desires and events.
   - Choose one of the seven strategies just described. Explain how you will use this strategy to assist you with managing the activities you listed.

AVOID PROCRASTINATION AND REDUCE STRESS

We all are guilty of **procrastination** at various times in our daily lives, be it paying a bill, looking for a summer job, writing a thank-you note, or doing the laundry. Still, constantly putting off responsibilities and tasks can be a major problem for college students, particularly for the important academic tasks of studying for exams, writing term papers, and keeping up with weekly reading assignments.

Procrastination causes undue stress, not to mention poorer performances. Underlying causes of procrastination are often complex and varied. However, having an awareness of *why* you are delaying a task often helps you tackle and complete it. The following list describes some of the common reasons why people procrastinate:

- **Being a perfectionist.** You want to be uncompromisingly perfect at this activity and don't want to do the activity unless you are able to achieve your unrealistically high expectations. Because perfection is essentially impossible to achieve, you continue to postpone the activity.
- **Avoiding failure.** You are concerned that you will fail or perform inadequately and, as a result, will disappoint yourself and others. Therefore, you procrastinate to steer clear of a poor grade—and subsequent failure.
- **Avoiding success.** You are concerned that, as a result of your achievements, you will be expected to handle additional, more difficult,

and/or burdensome responsibilities—responsibilities you simply don't want!

- **Being rebellious.** You disagree with *why* you should do an activity, dislike *who* you associate with the activity (such as an assignment from a professor you dislike), or dislike the *task itself* (such as reading from a text) and, therefore, put off the activity out of resentfulness or defiance.
- **Feeling overwhelmed.** You consider the task or assignment to be of overbearing proportions and don't know *where* or *how to* begin. Or you feel overburdened by multiple tasks and decisions and can't seem to get a handle on how to start tackling these activities.
- **Managing time poorly.** You don't plan ahead, use written schedules, or prioritize. You allow less significant tasks or events to get in the way.
- **Being lazy.** You want to avoid the effort and work involved in completing the task.

Critical
Thinking
Task

pause... *and reflect*

Identify one task, assignment, activity, or decision you should complete within the next week but you have been putting off.

Why are you putting off doing this? Use the list of reasons to describe the basis for your procrastination.

The following strategies will help you overcome procrastination:

1. **Know what you should accomplish.** You are more likely to complete a task that you clearly understand. Therefore, know expectations and what you are to undertake. If you are uncertain about what you should accomplish, *ask!*
2. **Determine deadlines.** Have a preset time limit for completing the whole task and, if appropriate, various steps of the task. People tend to follow deadlines established by other people (as opposed to self-imposed deadlines). Therefore, if your instructor does not provide a strict deadline, ask another person—a classmate, roommate, or peer tutor—to establish a reasonable written deadline for you.
3. **Use schedules/planners/calendars.** Write down *what* you want to do and *when* you will do it. You are more likely to accomplish a task that you write down.

4. **Prioritize.** Assign a level of importance to all tasks. Then categorize activities according to:
   - Will work on today.
   - Will work on today if time.
   - Will save for another day.

5. **Break a task into a series of steps.** Large tasks seem less overwhelming and more approachable if you view them as a series of steps, as opposed to a gigantic whole. At the very least, identify one step that you can do; then do it!

6. **Do the unpleasant task first.** Get the distasteful activity out of the way early, and then work on easier or more desirable activities.

7. **Change how you think about the task.** Instead of thinking of the activity as "dreaded" or "terrible," consider it as a practical means to an end, such as a course that completes a curriculum requirement, a grade to pass a course, or a term paper that gives you research and writing experience.

8. **Have fun with the activity.** See if you can be imaginative with the task, such as adding color and other creative elements to a written assignment. Or you can invent a game or competition for yourself, such as beating a previous time for completing the task or keeping pace with a classmate's score. Sharing and collaborating with other task-minded students can be an enjoyable method for dealing with difficult or disliked subjects.

9. **Establish rewards as personal incentives for completion.**
   - *Extrinsic rewards:* Compensate yourself by watching a favorite TV program, going out with friends, or buying a new CD.
   - *Intrinsic rewards:* Recognize the personal sense of satisfaction that you receive when you've completed the task. Relish the sense of accomplishment you feel when you are done and can check off the item!

"Time management is my absolute worst skill. I tend to procrastinate quite a bit. I get my work done but always just squeak in under the deadline. This year, however, I've been forcing myself to work when I *should*, rather than when I feel like it." —CHARISE

"Making written schedules actually helps me organize my day and seize wasted time. For example, instead of reading a magazine while waiting at the hair salon for my appointment, I read an assignment. When I feel organized my stress level drops tremendously. I feel on top of my assignments instead of overwhelmed by them." —JESS

Procrastination and Online Courses

The likelihood of procrastination increases if you are enrolled in distance education courses, which lack the built-in structure of weekly face-to-face meetings in a classroom. Additionally, when isolated at a computer, even routine assignments can seem tedious and time consuming, especially if you are uncomfortable with the technology. As course work piles up, you easily can feel overwhelmed, which leads to increased levels of procrastination. As a result, be especially mindful of monitoring your use of time when enrolled in online courses. These additional strategies will help you:

- Begin by getting an overview of course requirements for the whole semester. How much course work will you complete realistically each week? Mark these weekly units of work on your semester calendar.
- Be prepared to spend *more* time on online courses than you would on face-to-face courses. On your weekly schedule, block out generous amounts of time to read course materials and complete online assignments.
- Use your planner as a written log of what you intend to complete each day for the online course, and then cross off your daily accomplishments.

Plan ahead when enrolled in online courses. Use weekly schedules and daily planners to help monitor your productivity and maintain your momentum throughout the semester.

try it out!

Refer back to the task, assignment, or decision that you have been putting off (p. 30) and the nine strategies to overcome procrastination (pp. 30–31). Identify a strategy you will use to accomplish the task *this week*. Write a paragraph explaining the strategy. Be specific about what and how you will complete the task.

In one week's time, **Assess Your Success**:

Critical Thinking Task

- Did you complete the task? Did the strategy help you complete it? Explain.
- What other strategies will you use to focus your attention and energies on completing an unpleasant activity?

Personal Action Statement: Applying Time Management Techniques

s described in Chapter 1, a Personal Action Statement is a step-by-step written plan of a specific strategy—in this case a time management strategy—that you are committing yourself to do. Before developing your own Personal Action Statement, examine the three examples provided and answer these questions:

Critical Thinking Task

1. What are the differences among the plans?
2. Which students created plans that likely will result in successful outcomes? Why?

STUDENT A

1. I will study more for chemistry.
2. My greatest hurdle to achieving this is socializing.
3. I will eliminate this hurdle by socializing less.
4. My time plan for achieving this is soon—before the next test.
5. My reward for achieving this is A's in the class.

STUDENT B

1. I will study psychology for an hour after lunch each weekday.
2. My greatest hurdle to achieving this is afternoon soap operas on TV.
3. I will eliminate this hurdle by not watching *All of My Children* on Monday, Wednesday, and Friday and not watching *One Life to Live* on Tuesday and Thursday. This will leave me with an added hour each afternoon.
4. My time plan for achieving this is to begin on Monday.
5. My reward for achieving this is that I can start catching up with my reading assignments and thus feel better about the class and myself.

STUDENT C

1. I will use a calendar to write down due dates for all courses.
2. My greatest hurdle to achieving this is the lack of exact due dates in two of my subjects.
3. I will eliminate this hurdle by penciling in estimations of due dates in my planner.
4. My time plan for achieving this is to fill in dates this weekend.
5. My reward for achieving this is a better sense of organization in my daily life.

try it out!

Learning Style and Time Management

Being able to manage your time effectively is a crucial element of a successful system of study. By linking *how* you learn best (your learning style or preference) with *ways* to learn (strategies), you will be better able to refine time management methods that are effective for you.

1. Using Figure 2.4, in the right column, circle your dominant learning preference—visual, aural, read/write, or kinesthetic. If you are multimodal, that is, dominant in more than one modality, circle all that apply.
2. Refer to the time management strategies beside each of your preferences and place a check in the circles next to those that you do use regularly.
3. Next, identify a strategy that you do not use consistently but which would likely help you manage your time more effectively and efficiently for the upcoming week. Write a Personal Action Statement for that strategy, using the guidelines outlined in Chapter 1:
   - Is your Personal Action Statement a commitment for action?
   - Have you identified specific steps that make your plan manageable?
   - Have you been realistic and honest with yourself? Did you identify a step or strategy that you intend to use, as well as anticipated hurdles and rewards for yourself?
   - Have you put both thought and time into your Personal Action Statement?
4. At week's end, **Assess Your Success**. Refer back to your Personal Action Statement and evaluate your performance by answering the following questions:
   - Did you accomplish what you set out to do? Explain.
   - Were you able to overcome any obstacles? Think about your experience and how successful you were.
   - If you were not satisfied, what additional behaviors or techniques can you implement to make your system of time management effective and efficient for you? Will you try these new strategies in the near future?

| FIGURE 2.4 | *Time management strategies and learning preferences.* |

TIME MANAGEMENT STRATEGIES

TIME MANAGEMENT STRATEGIES	LEARNING PREFERENCES
○ Set up and use a weekly block schedule to create a "picture" of your week. ○ Use color to differentiate dates on the calendar and activities in your planner. ○ Use color and symbols to accentuate activities in your daily priority list, as well as each step needed to complete a project or paper. ○ Create an interest for routine assignments by setting personal goals and rewards and using a fanciful chart to keep track of your progress. ○ Use sticky notes as daily reminders. Place the notes in visible locations, such as on your computer, a bathroom mirror, refrigerator, or front door.	**Visual**
○ Get schedules for tutorials and group study sessions. Write the days and times in your planner. ○ Review notes and talk through assignments weekly with a classmate or study buddy. ○ Schedule time for Web chats. ○ Request auditory reminders from a roommate or family member. Give yourself daily reminders by talking out aloud to yourself.	**Aural**
○ Use a daily planner to write down daily appointments and tasks. ○ Determine appropriate amount of time to complete assignments for each subject. Write down starting and ending times for projects. ○ Write a due date earlier than actually needed. ○ Make daily to-do lists. As you accomplish each task, cross it off. ○ Keep your schedule, planner, and lists handy so you can review them regularly.	**Read/write**
○ Create a schedule that varies your activities. Consider ways to modify your approach toward tasks. For example, schedule time to work with others with routine assignments. ○ Allow extra time for lab work and application activities, especially for difficult subjects. ○ Schedule study slots for differing places, particularly locations that allow you to move about. ○ Break up longer assignments into workable steps, writing each step on a note card. ○ Post sticky notes with daily reminders.	**Kinesthetic**

Your Personal Action Statement

1. I will: _____

_____

_____

2. My greatest hurdle to achieving this is: _____

_____

_____

3. I will eliminate this hurdle by: _____

_____

_____

4. My time frame for achieving this is: _____

_____

_____

5. My reward for achieving this is: _____

_____

_____

STUDENT VOICES

"I really was not planning on this Personal Action Statement helping me much; however, I have to admit that it worked well. This was the first time I ever made a real schedule for myself, and I've now grown accustomed to using it. With a set schedule, I see the day as a whole and actually get more done, especially in those hidden time areas throughout the day. It's odd to me that something this small can totally change my whole perspective on how, where, and when I spend my time." —CHRIS

Conclusion

our decisions, and the subsequent consequences of these decisions, will determine how successful you are in college. Calendars, weekly schedules, and daily to-do lists are tools to assist you with the multitude of time management decisions. After all, your time is valuable, so use it wisely!

1. Establish a weekly routine early each semester.
2. Use a planner every day—write down what and when.
3. Put important dates on a calendar to know what events are coming up and not be caught off guard.
4. Make wise decisions about balancing your academic responsibilities with social and personal activities.
5. Be aware of when you are procrastinating, and then use strategies that assist you to begin and complete the task.
6. Take charge. Be proactive, and don't allow others to control how you use your time.

Comprehension Check

eturn to page 16. Without looking back through the chapter, provide a complete answer for each focus question. Then define each chapter term in your own words and provide an example.

C H A P T E R 3

Controlling Your Study Environment

FOCUS QUESTIONS

What is the connection between *when* you study and *where* you study?

Describe an ideal study environment for yourself.

CHAPTER TERMS

After reading this chapter, define (in your own words) and provide an example for each of the following terms:

- external distractions
- internal distractions

Controlling Your Study Environment: Three Essential Ingredients

Many hours of planned study time can be wasted if you are studying in an undesirable location, one that shifts your attention and efforts *away from* what you want to accomplish. Instead, assess your options and pinpoint a location that is conducive to quality study time. Take advantage of this location as much as possible. Thus alongside your planning of *when* you will study should be your planning of *where* to study. Include the following three ingredients in your plan:

1. Choose a suitable location.
2. Get organized.
3. Maximize concentration and minimize distractions.

Choose a Suitable Location

The following criteria will help you identify a desirable study location:

1. **Is this place *different from* where you sleep, eat, and socialize?** Although convenient, your dormitory room, apartment, or house often is full of distractions. Consider the multitude of distractions surrounding you in such a location—telephone, television, roommates, friends, family members, video games, a comfortable bed, personal chores, leisure activities, and so on. You are better off choosing a study place that you associate *only* with academics, such as a spare room, study lounge, empty classroom, tutorial center, or library carrel.

2. **Is this place away from direct foot traffic?** Choose a spot away from others. For example, a living room or a kitchen is often a high-traffic area, whereas other people rarely use an extra room in your house. In the library, an upper floor or corner table usually is better than the busy entranceway and main floor.

3. **Is this place readily accessible?** (Not accessible for other people who may distract you but accessible for *you!*) Find a location that is available and easy to get to when you are ready for study. Consider locations nearby—for example, a study lounge in a residence hall or student union, an empty room in a classroom building, an on-campus or off-campus library, or a desk in the basement.

4. **Does this place provide you with the needed flexibility?** Consider your environmental preferences. For instance, if you study best when you are able

to spread out materials, choose a location with tables, such as at a library. Or, if you prefer to listen to soft music when studying, choose a spare room or a friend's apartment. If you like to eat or drink when studying, consider an empty meeting room in the student union. In addition, consider your present lifestyle. Do you need to fit study time around family obligations or an outside job? Personal issues—such as health needs, family demands, employment, home responsibilities, and other commitments—can affect not only when you are able to study but also where you are able to study.

"I've been studying more frequently in a library study room or a classroom building. I've found that library study rooms have fewer people and are quieter during the day. During the evening, I study in an empty classroom—it is quiet, spacious, and I can open and close windows and have more control. I've gotten significantly more work done." —CHAD

try it out!

Critical Thinking Task

Rating Your Study Environment

Location A: What specific location do you most often use for study?

_____

Location B: What other location do you also use?

_____

Rate locations A and B by answering the four questions. Use the following point scale:

"Yes"	=	2 points		
"Somewhat"	=	1 point	Locations	
"No"	=	0 points	A	B

1. Is this place different from where you sleep, eat, and socialize?   ____ ____

2. Is this place away from direct foot traffic?   ____ ____

3. Is this place readily accessible?   ____ ____

4. Does this place provide you with the needed flexibility?   ____ ____

Total Points   ____ ____

Your total points for each location will be from a low of 0 to a high of 8. The higher your score, the more desirable the location should be for study.

8 or 7 points: An *excellent* place to concentrate and study. Use it often.

6, 5, or 4 points: A *fair* study location. Make some changes to lessen distractions.

3, 2, 1, or 0 points: A *poor* study location. Work on reducing distractions or move to another location.

Write an evaluation of your two locations. Consider these questions:

1. Which location had a higher score, A or B? Why?
2. What are your main distractions at each location?
3. Did your scores surprise you? Do you agree with the ratings?
4. What ways can you reduce distractions at each location?
5. What other locations would be worthwhile for study?

Get Organized: Increase Productivity and Reduce Stress

Organization is a vital component of effective, efficient study. When you organize your environment, you create an important sense of self-control and self-management, reducing your levels of anxiety and stress. An active take-charge approach toward arranging your surroundings often mirrors an active can-do approach toward your course work. Also, as you organize yourself and your surroundings, you will be *preparing* to work. You will discover that, when organized, you experience fewer missed appointments, forgotten assignments, lackluster test performances, and other day-to-day hassles and frustrations. As you become more productive, you'll notice a marked decrease in your daily worries and tensions. Following are some suggestions for organizing yourself.

Plan ahead. Keeping track of assignments, due dates, important events, and other short-term and long-term responsibilities is a fundamental aspect of personal planning. Use a written schedule—a planner, calendar, and daily to-do list—to prepare and plan in advance.

Have work supplies ready. Anticipate what you will need to complete assignments or activities. Keep your supplies in a central location, such as a desk or bookshelf. If you are a commuter student, keep your supplies in a portable container, such as a plastic storage box or tote bag. Store the container in your car or locker and carry what you need for classes, labs, or assignments.

Furthermore, set up a system for organizing and storing course materials. Some students prefer to have separate notebooks, folders, and storage bins for each course. Others use a large binder to organize notes and handouts, by subject, for the semester. Develop a system that makes sense to you and, importantly, provides an efficient means to access materials as you need them for each course.

SUPPLIES FOR COLLEGE STUDENTS

- ◯ Textbooks
- ◯ Supplemental CDs, study guides, lab guides, and so forth
- ◯ Notebooks for each course, either three-ring binders or spiral bound
- ◯ Labeled computer disks and CDs with carrying case, USB flash drive
- ◯ Pens, pencils, and highlighters
- ◯ Access to a computer and printer
- ◯ Paper—plain for printing and lined for notes
- ◯ Index cards
- ◯ Sticky notes
- ◯ Dictionary and thesaurus
- ◯ Daily planner and semester calendar, either paper or electronic format
- ◯ Stapler, paper clips, scissors, and hole puncher
- ◯ Wristwatch (Don't expect classrooms to have accurate clocks, and don't expect that you will be able to check your cell phone or other electronic device for the time.)
- ◯ Alarm clock
- ◯ Other: _____

Create order for yourself. An ordered environment will increase your overall work efficiency and productivity. A personal sense of neatness or orderliness differs from individual to individual. Know your preferences and tolerance in regard to cleanliness, room arrangement, and tidiness. Also, recognize that at times you'll be more productive if you rearrange or clean your study location *before* tackling your academic assignments.

try it out!

1. Review the list of college supplies. Mark which ones you already have and which ones you still need to get. Are there other supplies you should have for any of your classes this term? Where are you keeping the supplies so you can easily locate and use them?
2. Do a thorough inspection of your study environment. Characterize the degree of neatness or cleanliness that is important to you and results in your most productive work. Establish your environment accordingly; put supplies in proper receptacles, use shelves or drawers to store items, reduce clutter on your desk or tabletop, and create space to spread out work. If you have access to a camera, take a photo of the ordered setting; post the photo as a reminder of what your work area *should* look like!

Maximize Concentration and Minimize Distractions

Poor concentration results in inefficient use of your time. Distractions divert concentration and interrupt productive work. Therefore, the fewer the distractions, the better a location is for study. Distractions fall into two categories:

1. **Internal distractions** originate from within you. Examples are your mind wandering or your lack of motivation.
2. **External distractions** originate from a source outside of you. Examples are the TV, a computer, or noise. When establishing a suitable study location, consider this advice regarding common external distractions:
   - Study where noise levels are minimal. Research indicates that background noises from conversations, music, or other nearby activities can significantly impede thinking and concentration. Although some people prefer soft music or other low-level sounds when reading and studying, the rule of thumb is to avoid surrounding conversations and extra background noises.
   - Do not combine study with another activity, such as watching TV or preparing dinner. Research verifies that doing multiple activities decreases the quality and efficiency of learning. For example, if you study while instant-messaging friends, you might think you know the information. However, several days later when you need to *use* that information for a test, your accuracy of recall will be reduced because of the seemingly simple activity (instant messaging) that interrupted your primary task of studying.

STUDENT VOICES

"I commute to school and have explored suitable locations for study during blocks of time between classes. (The library is too quiet and too warm for me.) Sometimes I use the commuter lounge in the Student Union, especially in the mornings when fewer people are there. However, when I really need to concentrate, I find an unused room in a classroom building. I'm able to spread out my materials, eat my lunch, and move about when necessary." —MELISSA

"I used to study in my dorm room because it was comfortable and convenient, but I found this was not suitable. I got distracted easily, whether it was a distant radio or someone talking in the hall. Plus, I had a tendency to take many breaks. I now study at the library at a remote desk that has no radios, no people talking, and nothing else to occupy my time. For a break, I bring candy along with me. When I feel bored, I move to another desk in the library." —JOSH

try it out!

Controlling Distractions

Beside each distraction listed in Figure 3.1, note:

1. Is the distraction *external* or *internal?*
2. How often are you bothered by this distraction: *often, sometimes,* or *rarely?*
3. What are ways to *reduce* or *eliminate* this distraction?

Critical Thinking Task

pause... *and reflect*

1. Internal distractions tend to be more difficult to eliminate than do external distractions. Why?
2. Which type of distractions bothers you most, internal or external? Explain.
3. On the chart in Figure 3.1, check the circle next to your top three distractions. Consider several realistic, practical strategies for reducing each distraction. Ask for suggestions from others.

CW

Rating common distractions.

FIGURE **3.1**

Distractions	E = external I = internal	O = often S = sometimes R = rarely	Ways to Reduce or Eliminate
○ Phone			
○ Television			
○ Boredom			
○ Computer (e-mail, instant message, games, etc.)			
○ Roommates or family members			
○ Noise or music, including MP3 player			
○ Lack of interest			
○ Thinking about other activities or people			
○ People stopping by			
○ Laziness or lack of self-discipline			
○ Disorganization			
○ Worry			
○ Lack of goals for school or career			
○ Sleepiness			
○ Hunger			
○ Other responsibilities			
○ Not motivated			
○ *Any others?*			

try it out!

Critical Thinking Task

Learning Style and Study Environment

Establishing a study environment compatible with your preferences and tolerances sometimes requires you to think unconventionally, that is, away from the usual, more popular choices, which are living spaces (dorm room, bedroom, or kitchen) or the campus library. You want to create an environment that minimizes distractions while meeting your needs and preferences. The following steps will guide you when choosing a study location or organizational strategy compatible with your learning style.

1. Using Figure 3.2, in the right column circle your dominant learning preference, visual, aural, read/write, or kinesthetic. If you are multidimensional, that is, dominant in more than one modality, circle all that apply.

2. Refer to the strategies beside each of your preferences and place a check in the circles next to those that you *do* use regularly.

3. Identify a specific study location or organizational strategy that you will try *this week*. Write a Personal Action Statement for the strategy, using the guidelines outlined in Chapter 1:

   ○ Is your Personal Action Statement a commitment for action?

   ○ Have you identified specific steps that make your plan manageable?

   ○ Have you been realistic and honest with yourself? Did you identify a step or strategy that you intend to do, as well as anticipated hurdles and rewards for yourself?

   ○ Have you put both thought and time into your Personal Action Statement?

4. As you use this location, be attentive to how effectively you work and concentrate. At the end of the week, **Assess Your Success**. Refer back to your Personal Action Statement and evaluate your success by answering these questions:

   • Did you follow through with what you set out to do? Explain.

   • Were you able to overcome hurdles? How prevalent were external and internal distractions?

   • Did your reward provide a positive reinforcement for you?

   • Are you satisfied with this location? Does it seem to fit your particular needs and lifestyle? What additional changes do you want to make? Is there a location that might be superior you will try?

Study location/organizational strategies and learning preferences.

FIGURE 3.2

STUDY LOCATION AND ORGANIZATIONAL STRATEGIES	LEARNING PREFERENCES
○ Choose a study location free of noises and other distractions so that you can fully concentrate on visualizing information. ○ Be creative with modifying your favorite study location—change posters, add pictures and colorful decorations, rearrange furniture, and make other novel modifications to make your space visually appealing to you. ○ Create an open, uncluttered study space for yourself. ○ Organize your course materials using color-coded notebooks, folders, and bins.	**Visual**
○ Choose a location where you can study out loud with others, such as a lounge or an empty classroom. If by yourself, go to a room where you can close the door and talk out loud to yourself as you study. ○ Go to a tutorial center or homework helper location to discuss your subject matter with others. ○ Obtain CDs or audiotapes that accompany course materials. Use a tape recorder and audiocassettes or a laptop computer with an embedded microphone to record lectures. Also, record yourself as you recite out loud.	**Aural**
○ Create a structured, traditional study environment for yourself with a desk or table to write on, notepaper, and supplies organized according to subject. ○ Obtain supplies so you can rewrite and reorganize notes after class. For each course, have a three-ring binder to hand-write notes. Get a three-hole punch to add course handouts in the binder. ○ If using a computer to word-process notes, organize notes in folders according to topics and courses.	**Read/write**
○ Choose a study location that allows you to move about freely, such as an empty classroom or lab room. ○ Purposely try new and different spaces for study. ○ Be creative with organizing your favorite study location—rearrange furniture to allow movement and get storage bins for course materials. ○ Obtain any interactive CDs, videos, and lab manuals that accompany course materials. ○ Have index cards of varying sizes, colors, and shapes. Keep the cards organized by subject in storage containers or accordion folders.	**Kinesthetic**

Your Personal Action Statement

1. I will: _____
   _____
   _____

2. My greatest hurdle to achieving this is: _____
   _____
   _____

3. I will eliminate this hurdle by: _____
   _____
   _____

4. My time frame for achieving this is: _____
   _____
   _____

5. My reward for achieving this is: _____
   _____

Conclusion

Be mindful of *where* you study. Work at creating a suitable study environment, a setting that maximizes productive use of your study time. Improve your concentration by minimizing both external and internal distractions. Finally, establish an ordered, uncluttered work space for yourself to improve your productivity while reducing your stress.

Comprehension Check

Return to page 38. Provide a complete answer for each focus question. Then define each chapter term in your own words and provide an example.

CHAPTER 4

Active Listening and Note Taking

FOCUS QUESTIONS

Why is active listening important?

How are active listening and selective listening similar and different?

CHAPTER TERMS

After reading the chapter, define (in your own words) and provide an example for each of the following terms:

- active listening
- listening cues
- nonverbal cues
- selective listening
- verbal cues

ESSENTIAL INGREDIENTS College Studying

Active Listening: Three Essential Ingredients

Listening to and hearing information are not the same. You perceive sounds when you *hear* information, whereas *listening* implies more than just a physical act. Listening is an active process—in addition to hearing information, you are *thinking* about the information. Good listening requires alertness and energy; you must pay attention and focus on *what* information is being presented, *why* you should know the information, and *how* you should represent the information in your notes. Therefore, **active listening** involves many decisions on the listener's part. When done well, note taking will help you listen actively.

You will discover that, on a typical exam, the majority of information comes from material covered in class. Therefore, take notes! The purpose of class notes is twofold: To help you *understand* class information, and to help you *remember* class information.

Active listening and note-taking skills are fundamental to college success. The following essential ingredients added before, during, and after each class will maximize your proficiency as a student:

1. Prepare before class.
2. Listen and take notes during class.
3. Follow up after class.

Prepare Before Class

The most essential strategy is to *go to class*. The importance of class attendance cannot be overstated. Most of the information that will be on tests, as well as directions for assignments and papers, are covered in class. Copying someone else's notes is not the same as personally being in class to observe, listen, and ask questions. Of course, illness and personal emergencies do arise. If you are unable to attend class, let the professor know via an e-mail or phone message. *Before the next class*, find out what was covered in class and any assignments you missed.

Prepare yourself physically for class; resting and eating well will improve your listening concentration. In addition, bring supplies, texts, and completed assignments. If your instructor places notes on a Website or campus network drive, print out and take the notes with you to class. Try to arrive a few minutes early to get seated and ready to listen and take notes. You may find the following list of appropriate supplies helpful in preparing for class.

BRING APPROPRIATE SUPPLIES

- **Paper**
    - A *loose-leaf paper and binder* provides you with the most flexibility. Use this type if you print copies of lecture information from a Website, if you have handouts to insert within your notes, or if your instructor jumps from topic to topic during the lecture. Also, use loose-leaf paper if you prefer to spread out pages for an ordered overview of a topic or time period.
    - A *spiral-bound notebook* tends to be the more convenient type of notebook because the paper is already packaged for you. If your instructor presents information in an orderly, straightforward manner you might favor a spiral-bound notebook, especially one with pockets for handouts.

- **Writing Utensils**
    - *Ink pens* help you write faster and more clearly. Also, your writing will last longer with ink pens rather than with lead pencils.
    - *Lead pencils* generally will make your writing slower and lighter. However, use lead pencils if you do a lot of erasing, such as in a problem-solving mathematics or chemistry course.
    - *Colored markers, pens, and pencils* can be used to provide *emphasis* for key words and phrases.

Laptop computers are an increasingly popular tool for classroom note taking. They can be advantageous if you type faster than you write, although with a tablet PC you can write notes by hand. The word processing program can aid you with highlighting important ideas during class time and organizing your notes. In classrooms with wireless Internet connections, you will be able to access course-related Websites and PowerPoint materials for in-class discussions and activities.

But the lure of the Internet also creates a major disadvantage when you use computers during class time. You might easily check e-mail, surf the Web, or watch online videos, all the while insisting that you are paying attention to the class lecture. Research confirms that this type of multitasking *does* affect concentration. Although you might be very accustomed to juggling a number of technological tasks, in the learning environment of a classroom active listening is best accomplished when your attention and thoughts are directed only toward class topics.

BE FAMILIAR WITH THE MATERIAL

- **Read, or at least skim through, text assignments or online information** to provide background and better understanding of ideas to be presented in the lecture. Consider keeping your text open during class for easy referral when (1) the instructor's lecture parallels the text information, (2) the instructor mentions the text frequently, or (3) the text presents the subject matter in a clear, easily understood format.

- **Look over notes from the previous lecture** to refresh your memory about where the lecture ended and what topics were covered. This refresher provides a transition between class sessions and helps focus your attention on the current day's topic.
- **Look over written or online assignments** that the instructor likely will refer to during class.

Critical
Thinking
Task

pause... *and reflect*

1. What should you do *before* class for each course you are enrolled in this term? Using Figure 4.1, fill in the chart indicating your preparation for each subject.
2. A universal recommendation is for students to choose a seat in the front of each classroom. When sitting in the front, you will be able to hear and see better. Name two other reasons why you should choose a seat in the front of a classroom.

FIGURE 4.1 *Preparation by subject.*

Subject	Supplies needed for class	Type of preparation for class

"Two years ago I had one exceptionally bad semester where I did nothing at all (this included skipping most classes, some tests, and two finals). Afterward, I was on academic probation and then dismissed from college. I worked for two years. Now I'm trying college again with a different attitude. One thing that has influenced my performance is that I figured out what each class hour costs me. I added tuition, books, meals, housing, and all fees and divided the total by the number of class hours in a semester (256 for me). This semester, each class I miss costs me about $24.97! I figure since the class is paid for, I'll go and get my $25 worth!   —MICHAEL

Listen and Take Notes During Class

Creating notes is a major component of active listening and involvement during class. Note taking helps you be more alert, discriminate important points, and organize information, all of which are keys to understanding and remembering. Not only is note taking important during lectures but also when listening to course-related movies, videos, and online DVDs. Take into account the following five factors as you listen and take notes during a class session.

1. LISTEN SELECTIVELY

Focus on *ideas*, not just words. Throughout the lecture, continually ask yourself, "What are the important points that the instructor is trying to get across?" Then write down enough information to help you understand those points. **Selective listening** involves an awareness of what is and is not important enough to write down. Thus selective listening requires active decision making on your part. Instead of writing down everything the instructor says, choose main ideas and corresponding supporting points, including explanations and examples. As you listen, ask yourself questions, which will help you to pick out noteworthy ideas:

Critical Thinking Task

- "What is the *topic*?"
- "What do I need *to know* about the topic?"
- "Why is this topic *important*?"
- "What is an *example* of the topic?"
- "How did this event or procedure *come about*?"

If you are unsure of how much information to write down in your notes, it is best to err on the side of writing *too much* rather than *too little*. When you review notes after class, you will have the opportunity to highlight key points while eliminating redundant information.

During lectures, instructors give many clues as to what is and is not important, termed **listening cues.** Keep in mind: If your instructor thinks an idea is important, that idea likely will be on an upcoming test; thus you want to capture the idea and related information in your notes.

Verbal cues are what your instructor *says* that signals an idea is important enough to write down. For example, your instructor *repeats information* (making sure you hear and write it down), *pauses or slows down* when talking (giving you time to write down information), or *talks louder* (ensuring that you hear).

Nonverbal cues are what your instructor *does* that indicates an idea is important. For example, your instructor *uses hand gestures* (to help explain important information), *points to words on the board* (to make sure you see and write the information), or walks among students *looking at their notes* (to see if they are writing down correct information).

Critical
Thinking
Task

pause.... *and reflect*

What verbal and nonverbal cues do your instructors use to signal important ideas? Target a course in which you will be listening to lectures for the upcoming week. In class, be attentive to your instructor's cues. Keep a diary of your observations for the week.

Verbal cues:

_____

_____

Nonverbal cues:

_____

_____

2. TAKE CONCISE NOTES

In many classes, you will be quickly writing down numerous ideas; therefore, use as few words as you need to communicate these ideas. Here are some tips to help you be concise and succinct.

Write in phrases, not whole sentences. Focus on those words that convey *ideas* within statements. What words are necessary to write down to communicate these ideas? You can usually eliminate adjectives, adverbs, prepositions, and conjunctions and still get across the core meaning. Therefore, in your note taking, focus on the *subject* or *topic* and *what you need to know* about the topic, as illustrated here:

Instructor says, "Both external and internal distractions contribute to inadequate attention spans of college students attending large introductory-level lecture classes."

You write, "external & internal distract's ⟶ poor attention of students in lecture classes"

After class: You go over what you wrote and |BOX| the terms "external and internal distractions" for *emphasis* and add *examples* for *clarity*:

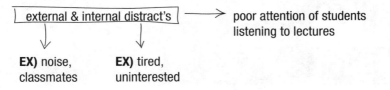

EX) noise,   **EX)** tired,
classmates   uninterested

Use abbreviations and symbols. Accustom yourself to using abbreviations and symbols when taking notes. Both will help you reduce the quantity of writing necessary to get ideas across on paper. Repeat abbreviations and symbols within your notes so they become familiar and identifiable to you. Here are some techniques for shortening words:

- Use beginning letters of words or phrases:
    "without" = w/o
    "overdose" = OD
    "sign on" = S.O.
    "as soon as possible" = asap
- Use beginning syllables:
    "anthropology" = anthro
    "demonstration" = demo
    "approximately" = approx
- Remove vowels because the tendency is to recognize words by consonants:
    "explosion" = explsn
    "check" = chck
    "notebook" = notebk
- Use the beginning and end of words:
    "abbreviations" = abbrev's
    "continued" = cont'd
    "additional" = add'l

- Use common characters and symbols:
    - ? = "I don't understand"
    - @ = "at"
    - ⟶ = "linked to or causes"
    - * or ! = "important"
- Use mathematical signs:
    - > < represent "greater than/less than"
    - = means "equal to"
    - # for "number"
    - ~ means "approximately"
    - + for "and"

try it out!

Practice your note-taking skills: Imagine you are listening to the following passage in a class. Create your class notes on a separate sheet of paper. Be *selective* (focus on important ideas), and be *concise* (write in phrases and use abbreviations and symbols).

Consider the difference between "hearing" and "listening." Hearing is simply the physical function of perceiving sound, whereas listening involves thoughtful attention to those sounds as received by an individual. There are three types of listening: casual, attentive, and evaluative. Casual listening is when one listens to understand but not necessarily remember. Examples include listening to a friend talk or to the radio or TV. Most of everyday listening is classified as casual listening. On the other hand, a high degree of remembering is a distinctive characteristic of attentive listening, which involves more thought, alertness, and energy than does casual listening. Most of college students' classroom listening should be of this type. Bear in mind that note taking helps an individual to listen attentively. The type of listening requiring the most thought process and energy is evaluative listening. For this category, not only does the listener want to remember, but he also intends to assess information heard. For instance, in a literature course, the instructor gives an assignment to attend a poetry reading and write a critique of a recited poem. The student would be listening to the poem with the intent of assessing critically—thus evaluative listening. Taking written notes strengthens one's evaluative listening skills.

Afterward, compare your notes with the sample notes in Figure 4.2.

3. BE CLEAR

Make your notes understandable enough for *you*. After class, you will review the day's lesson; at this point, you will be able to clarify ideas further by rewriting information, adding explanations and examples, and integrating text material.

Thus be generous with paper as you take class notes. Avoid cramming topics together on the pages. Instead, leave ample spaces between ideas, especially when you know that information is missing. Consider writing on one side of the paper only so that you will have the back to add information, if needed.

In addition, standardize a method for organizing your notes. Always place the subject, date, and topic at the start of the day's notes. As you write, consider the arrangement of ideas. Write main ideas at the left margin and then indent supporting ideas and details. Underline or capitalize headings. Use numbers or letters to itemize separate points. Where appropriate, categorize ideas and add formulas and other visual aids. Include examples from class, and allow space to add more examples and explanations later. Figure 4.2 exemplifies concise, clear, well-organized notes.

Sample class notes.   FIGURE **4.2**

Learning Strategies — Oct. 9	
<u>HEARING vs. LISTENING</u> (cont'd)	Subject, date, and topic at top of page.
I. <u>Difference</u> between:	
** Important ──→ know **	Visual emphasis.
A. Hear'g – physical act of perceiv'g sound	
B. Listen'g – involves thought & attention	Use of abbreviations and symbols.
II. <u>3 types Listen'g</u>:	
A. Casual –need to understand, not remember	Topic in headings with supporting details itemized beneath.
(used most often)	
ex.→ talk w/ friend	
B. Attentive –high am't. remembering, ↑ thought	
(notetakg helps)	Illustrations and examples.
ex.→ in lecture class	
	Spaces between topics. Extra space to add information after class.
C. Evaluative –most thought & energy b/c assessing	
(note taking helps)	
* see chapter 4 in text	References to text.

4. BE ACCURATE

To ensure that you are representing the ideas accurately within your notes, do the following:

- **Examine your notes *soon* after class.** Go back over your notes while the information from the class is still fresh in your mind, usually within 24 hours after the class.
- **Consult your textbook, lab manual, or other reference source.** If you notice a discrepancy between your class notes and the text or other written source, seek clarification from your instructor, graduate assistant, or a peer educator.
- **Go over class information with peers.** One of the most effective means for review of class notes is regular attendance at peer-led study groups. If you are unable to locate formal study/review groups, establish your own by inviting classmates (who are serious, capable students) to join you weekly for collaborative review.

Likewise for an online course: Seek classmates to review notes and ask questions of one another. Instant messenger can be an excellent tool for online study groups.

5. PAY ATTENTION

Paying attention is a key element of effective listening and note taking. Daydreaming is a problem for many students. Physically being in class is ineffectual if you are not also mentally attending to class.

The foremost tactic for maintaining your concentration in class is willfully wanting to pay attention. In the nearby "Student Voices," notice Bernice's choice of the word *intend* when describing how she improved her alertness in her accounting course.

STUDENT VOICES

"I intended to pay closer attention in accounting class. I did have my moments of daydreaming, but, for the most part, I did listen and followed along with the material being presented. I actually knew how to do homework problems; it was a nice feeling!" —BERNICE

Personal determination plays a huge role in attentiveness and concentration, even in boring or undesirable situations.

Participate in class. *Answer* questions. *Comment* on topics. *Ask* for clarification. Your involvement and participation can enliven a class lecture and keep you more alert.

The anonymous nature of an online course makes active participation especially important. Know when your instructor is available online so you can initiate e-mails and ask for feedback and clarification throughout the course. Also, be sure to participate regularly in electronic discussion boards and chat rooms for the course.

Sit up front. Being able to see and hear better should help you to pay attention. Also, knowing you are highly visible to your instructor can motivate you to be more alert and involved in class.

Create physical movement. Bring a caffeinated drink (if permitted). Chewing on gum or candy can help keep your mind activated. Switch colored pens. Applying gentle pressure to stimulation points on your body—top of your head, sides of the back of your neck, or back of your hand between your thumb and forefinger—can aid in keeping you alert. Even slight movements, such as wiggling your leg, can help you stay awake and focused.

"There is no substitute for taking your own notes. Note taking helps me to pay attention to a lecture as well as organize and remember the ideas. As every student quickly learns, merely sitting through a class is not enough to ensure good grades." —OLIVIA

"Unlike in the past, I now look over my notes more frequently and actually read the text as assigned. Now I feel *much more* comfortable during class discussions since I am more familiar with the material, instead of hearing it for the first time right there in class." —JUSTIN

STUDENT VOICES

A NOTE ABOUT WEB NOTES

A growing number of instructors are posting lecture notes, often in the form of an outline or Microsoft PowerPoint presentation, on a Website, or on campus computers with a common network. Have these notes with you in class, either hard copies or copies on your laptop computer. Be prepared to do additional note taking in class as a means to supplement and clarify information. Be alert to your instructor's emphasis of key points using verbal and nonverbal cues. As you listen, insert information and examples that help explain ideas. Circle or highlight key terms and phrases. Use your system of abbreviations and symbols to illuminate important material. During class, you are beginning to create a study guide for yourself, as detailed in the following section. (After class, you still will need to review your notes and continue with your study guide; see Figures 4.3 and 4.4.)

FIGURE **4.3**   *Study guide with text references and summary.*

BIOLOGY   4/11
              class notes – Chap. 15, Carboxylic Acids

Carboxylic Acids contain the _carboxyl grp._
        O   – a hydroxyl grp. Bonded to carbonyl C
        ‖
R – C – OH – Is polar, meaning it will form H+ bonds causing high
                melting/boiling pts.

Names: ⎡see CHART in CHAP 15⎤
1) Methanoic acid – ant & bee stings
2) Ethanoic acid – vinegar ————————→   ⎡Will hydrogen bond cause
3) Propanoic acid – dairy products   high melt'g/boil'g pts?⎤
4) Butanoic acid – rancid butter
5) Oxalic acid – rhubarb
6) Citric acid – sour taste in lemon
7) Lactic acid – sour milk

Naming C.A.'s   ⎡full rules on p. 437⎤
* oic ending
* the C on carboxylic acid is #1
* for anions, change to "-ate" ending & omit "acid"

DIMER – special H+ bonding structure CA's may take on.

   ⎡Note structure on p. 438 **GOOD TEST QUESTION**⎤

SUMMARY:
Carboxylic Acids contain the carboxyl group. They are long, straight changes
called fatty acids from hydrolysis of dietary fats. There are seven types,
named according to rules of oic, C on carboxylic acid & changing -ate to
acid. A dimer is a special H+ structure.

STUDY GUIDE created AFTER class
The following are after-class additions:

1. Numbers to organize listing

2. Additions from related text chapter

3. A written summary of key points   [Notes contributed by Adrienne Runk]

Study guide for Web-based notes.   FIGURE **4.4**

| Web Notes | | INTRODUCTION to GEOLOGY | | | Week Two |
| | | CHARACTERISTICS OF SEDIMENTARY ROCKS | | | |

Type of Rock	Sediment	Environment	Mineral	Chemical Composition	OTHER INFO
LIMESTONE	Calcite Shells (alike) ↓↑	Shallow warm oceans	Calcite (alike) ↓↑	CaCO3 (alike) ↓↑	1. carbonate sand & mud 2. has to be shallow & warm b/c organisms making the shells don't live in cold water 3. calcite dissolves in cold water
CHALK	Microscopic Calcite Shells	Quiet deep sea floor; organisms fall to the bottom when they die	Calcite	CaCO3	**SIMILAR to Limestone
CHERT	Tiny Silica Shells	↓↑ (alike) Quiet deep sea floor; colder water	Opal Quartz	SiO2	Siliceous Sediment ↓↑ (vs.)
EVAPORITES	Gypsum Halite	Dried lakes or oceans	Bypsum Halite Anhydrite	Gypsum-CaCO3 Halite-NaC1	1. Evaporite Sediment 2. made in desert climates—Death Valley, Persian Gulf
PEAT/COAL	Plant Debris	Swamp Bog	Coal Oil Gas	Carbon	1. pure organic matter 2. Function: preserves organic matter by keeping animals out that would eat it

Study Questions:
1. What are the 5 types of sedimentary rock?
2. Describe the composition, environment, and key features of each.
3. Which types are similar?

During class the student:
1. Added last column ("OTHER INFO") to write additional information.
2. Added phrases linking certain types: "↓↑ (alike)".
3. Highlighted the names of rocks and other terms.

After class the student:
4. Wrote three study questions on the back of the paper.

Follow Up After Class

Review your class notes and create a study guide for yourself. To reduce the progression of forgetting, incorporate this step within 24 hours after a class. By immediately reviewing, you will be checking your understanding of class material. Do the following as you go over your notes:

- Highlight key words or phrases.
- Condense information.
- Fill in incomplete material.
- Add explanations and examples in your own words.
- Refer to text material.
- Summarize key points.
- Think about what you need to know for the upcoming quiz, exam, or discussion, and develop questions for yourself.

By adding, condensing, emphasizing, and organizing lecture information, you will be creating a valuable study guide for yourself. Figures 4.3 and 4.4 illustrate differing study guides. By reviewing and *doing something* with notes soon after class, you are immediately integrating study with note taking. That is, you are learning the subject matter while it is still fresh in your mind. This strategy is considerably more effective and efficient than the usual method of only reviewing class notes days—or even hours—before the exam. Because reviewing notes and creating a study guide *soon after class* is pivotal for understanding and remembering class information, incorporate this study strategy into your weekly routine from the beginning of the semester.

Review weekly. For an overview of the subject matter, each week skim through the study guides you created from your class notes. This will help you see connections among topics. Reinforce these connections by saying key ideas out loud.

Use academic support services. Participate in group study and review sessions regularly. If you don't understand something, ask your instructor, graduate student, or peer tutor for an explanation.

Use the Cornell note-taking system. A popular method of note taking is the Cornell system, developed at Cornell University over 40 years ago (Pauk, 2001, pp. 236–241). A key component of this system is the wide formal columns on each sheet of notepaper used for after-class study guides and review:

- A $2\frac{1}{2}$-inch cue column on the left side of the paper to develop questions
- A 2-inch strip at the bottom of the paper to write a summary

The steps for the Cornell note-taking system are as follows:

1. During class, take notes using the 6-inch space on the right side of the notepaper.

Cornell system of note taking.   FIGURE **4.5**

2½"	6"	World Politics 3/17

Chap. 7 "POWER"

Define "power" in international affairs.
Power in Internat'l. Relations/ ⟶ ability of an actor (?) on internat'l stage to use tangible + intangible resources + assets to influence outcomes of internat'l events.

actor can be a nation or leader/agent

POWER is:

What is an "actor" on international stage?
1. Means by which internat'l actors deal w/ each other
2. Product of tangible materials & intangible behavioral resources

What are the four purposes of "power"?
tangible is concrete MATERIALS; intangible is how nation/agent ACTS

Give examples of tangible vs. intangible resources.
3. Means for achieving influence over others
4. Attempt to shape outcome of internat'l events to maintain or improve internat'l political environ.

How does "force" differ from "power"?
~ Power is NOT Force ~ force is at extreme end of continuum of choices available to a nation when agents strive to manipulate outcomes of events.

2" | POWER in international relations is when a nation or a leader influences international events via resources. Power has 4 functions; power differs from FORCE, which is extreme manipulation.

[The after-class additions are boxed in the above notes.]
1. *During class,* the student took notes on the six-inch right side of paper.
2. *Soon afterward,* the student went back over notes: clarified terms (*actor, tangible, intangible*) and underlined/highlighted to emphasize key concepts/terms;
3. Created five questions in the "cue column";
4. Covered the notes and recited answers to each question;
5. Wrote a summary in the bottom 2-inch space;
6. Reviewed immediately; and then
7. Reflected on the material's overall importance.

2. Soon after class, go back over your notes, filling in information.
3. Use the cue column to develop questions based on each key idea.
4. Cover the body of your notes (in the 6-inch area) with a sheet of paper. Recite the answer to each question in the cue column, checking your answer by uncovering the body of your notes. Repeat this step until your answers are correct.
5. Use the 2-inch space at the bottom to write a concise summary of ideas on the page.
6. Review your notes right away to reinforce the material.
7. Reflect about the importance of the overall ideas.

Figure 4.5 illustrates the Cornell system of note taking.

try it out!

Target a course in which you take many and frequent class notes. Within 24 hours after each class for the next week, review your notes and create a study guide using the strategies illustrated in Figures 4.2, 4.3, 4.4, and 4.5.

Dealing with Difficult Lecturers

igure 4.6 summarizes common difficulties that students encounter in lectures, as well as suggestions for dealing with the difficulties and adapting to instructors' styles. What information can you add?

Critical Thinking Task

pause... *and reflect*

Consider the instructors for your classes. Which instructors have exhibited characteristics that you found to be difficult to listen to or distracting? Use Figure 4.6 to identify your instructors' characteristics and accompanying suggestions.

• Which suggestions will you use for that class?
• What additional suggestions can you add?

Use Figure 4.7 to keep track of suggestions and adaptations for the classes you have identified.

Dealing with difficult lecturers.   FIGURE **4.6**

Instructor Characteristics	Suggestions for Students
Talks over students' heads; uses complex words and ideas.	○ Review chapter to be covered. ○ Ask lots of questions. ○ Talk with the instructor outside of class to seek explanations.
Jumps from topic to topic; unorganized.	○ Reorganize notes *after* each class. ○ Have a three-ring binder with the aim of using a separate sheet of paper for each topic; reorganize the pages after class. ○ Leave room within the notes or use the back of the notepaper, so you have space to reorganize your notes and fill in details after class. ○ Record (with permission), and use the tape to help you reorganize notes, by topic, after class. ○ Read and review the textbook before and after class to give you background information about organization of topics. ○ Ask lots of questions in and out of class.
Talks too fast.	○ Review notes after every class—use the text to fill in what you missed. ○ Use tape recorder (with permission); listen to the tape after class, and fill in parts you missed. ○ Jot down *only* key points and ideas—leave spaces to fill in added details after class. ○ See the instructor during office hours to review what you missed or don't fully understand. ○ Review notes regularly with other students. ○ Ask the instructor to slow down and/or to repeat information.
Talks with a foreign accent.	○ Sit in the front of the room near the instructor. ○ Talk to the instructor one on one; this will help you get used to the instructor's manner of speech. ○ Ask the instructor to repeat information. ○ Listen carefully and ask for visual reinforcements, such as the use of overheads, the board, and handouts. ○ Review notes regularly with other students.

(continued)

FIGURE **4.6** *Continued.*

Instructor Characteristics	Suggestions for Students
Presents information in a lifeless, boring manner.	○ Sit near the instructor. ○ Bring colorful supplies—at least create lively notes for yourself! ○ Ask questions and urge classmates to ask questions to enliven presentation.
Condescending or impersonal toward students.	○ See if you can talk to and form a relationship with the instructor. ○ Ignore it. ○ Seek help and personal affirmation out of class.
Skips over important topics that likely will be on tests.	○ Bring up those topics; ask questions. ○ Ask the instructor to review major topics on the test.
Gives a large amount of information.	○ Dissect information when reviewing notes after class. ○ Go over information in study groups.
Repeats topics too much, or students are too familiar with topics.	○ Ask questions to possibly move the instructor ahead. ○ Ask about related topics. ○ Use markers or colored pens while in class to reinforce and emphasize major concepts within your notes. ○ Look ahead to future topics.
Doesn't want to be bothered explaining material.	○ Be persistent; keep asking questions. ○ Personally talk to the instructor after class—try to establish a working relationship. ○ Seek help from a tutor or another student.
Is unprepared for class or online instruction.	○ Go to tutoring to fill in gaps. ○ Read and study the textbook before and after class. ○ Ask lots of questions and show interest; this might spur the instructor to prepare better for class.
Doesn't respond to e-mails or give feedback about online assignments.	○ Find out the instructor's office hours. Call during that time or make a face-to-face appointment. ○ Leave a clear message on the instructor's answering machine or with the office secretary.

Others:

Chart for tracking suggestions.   FIGURE **4.7**

INSTRUCTOR/SUBJECT	STRATEGIES

try it out!

Critical
Thinking
Task

Learning Style and Active Listening/Note Taking

By combining knowledge, time, and practice, you are developing a system of listening and note taking that is most effective for you. Assess your strategies regularly: Do you need to improve class preparation? Do you want to modify how you listen or where you sit in a particular class? Should you be trying a different format for note taking? By combining the elements of active listening and note taking with your preferences for learning, you will be able to fine-tune your approaches toward in-class listening and note taking.

1. Using Figure 4.8, in the right column circle your dominant learning preference—visual, aural, read/write, or kinesthetic. If you are multi-dimensional, that is, dominant in more than one modality, circle all that apply.

2. Refer to the listening and note-taking strategies beside each of your preferences and place a check in the circles next to those that you do use regularly.

3. Identify a specific strategy that you will try this week. Refer to the examples in Figure 4.9 for suggestions, and then, write a Personal Action Statement for that strategy.

4. At the end of the week, **Assess Your Success:**
   - Did you follow through and reward yourself accordingly? Explain.
   - Did the hurdle materialize, and did you manage it effectively?
   - Examine your habits before, during, and after a class. Describe the changes you need to make.

STUDENT VOICES

"I know reviewing class notes is important for learning. However, with a husband, a full-time job, two aging parents, not to mention household duties, I've always had problems finding the time. However, lately I've done two things that have greatly helped: (1) Between classes, I review what happened by talking (silently) to myself, and (2) When I'm in the car, I review by listening to a tape of the day's lecture. —KYLIE

Active listening strategies and learning preferences.   FIGURE **4.8**

LISTENING AND NOTE-TAKING STRATEGIES	LEARNING PREFERENCES

○ Before class, skim through the chapter and read the summary. This will assist you to see the whole picture of the lecture topic.

○ During class, sit up front so that you can readily see the board, screens, overhead transparencies, and other visual presentations.

○ Form a mental "picture" of ideas being presented during a lecture. Write down associations, relationships, and illustrations in your notes.

○ Use three-ring binders and write on one side of the paper. Leave generous space between ideas in your notes. Have a least two colors of pens for use during class note taking.   **Visual**

○ After class, add visual emphasis by highlighting and color-coding key concepts, terms, and phrases within your notes. Use differing fonts for typed notes.

○ Reduce your class notes by creating visual summaries, such as charts, graphs, and timelines, that show the organization of information and relationships among ideas.

○ While reviewing lecture notes, picture how the information fits into text readings.

○ Participate in class; ask and answer questions. For online course work, participate in discussion groups.

○ If appropriate, ask permission to tape the instructor's lecture. Use a high-quality tape recorder or a laptop computer with an embedded microphone. After class, use the recording to review areas of the lecture that you are unsure about.

○ Leave spaces when taking notes so that you can fill in missing information when you review later.

○ Because you prefer to listen, your class notes may be incomplete. After class expand your notes by referring to the textbook, listening to an audio recording, or talking with classmates.   **Aural**

○ When reviewing your lecture notes, recite out loud to yourself. Record yourself and listen while in your car or use your MP3 player.

○ Participate in group lecture review sessions. Compare and discuss notes with others, especially classmates with "read/write" preferences.

○ Teach others; this will clarify information and reinforce what you know.

○ See the instructor before or after class or during office hours for answers to your questions.

(continued)

FIGURE **4.8** *Continued.*

○ Class lectures and discussion are often your strength; thus (1) go to every class, and (2) use the in-class information as a basis for understanding the course subject matter.

○ Because reading is a strong suit, read the corresponding text material *before* class as a way to strengthen your understanding of the subject matter.

○ Create an outline of text information. Bring the outline to class to use as a reference for lecture material.

○ Add your own notes to PowerPoint and online lecture materials. Download and write on the hard copy during class. Type your notes if using a laptop or write if using a tablet PC.

Read/write

○ Prepare a written weekly log of when you will review notes soon after class and complete course assignments.

○ Review your notes after class: Rewrite or retype your outline, summarize key information, create questions that identify the important ideas.

○ For online course work, e-mail your professor regularly. E-mail online classmates about questions you have and participate in discussions.

○ If a laboratory experience is attached to the course, *go*. Take notes, ask questions, and be actively involved. Use the lab or field experience as a basis for understanding and remembering course concepts.

○ For laboratory work, use a laptop computer to record progress on experiments in real time. Review after class.

○ Preview the related lab assignment *before* the next class. This can help you better understand the lecture.

○ Sit at the front of a classroom where you will encounter fewer distractions. During the lecture, move your legs and use your hands to take notes.

○ Use a three-ring binder for course notes. Write on one side so that you can spread out the sheets of paper when studying.

Kinesthetic

○ During a lecture, focus on key ideas, jot down important words and phrases, use abbreviations and symbols, and indicate any information that is unclear to you.

○ Add concrete and relevant explanations, examples, analogies, and case studies within your notes.

○ Use your *senses* when reviewing: recite aloud; move around; add visual, colorful emphasis to your notes; participate in a study group to discuss and hear others talk about the subject matter.

○ When reviewing notes after class, create a skit using terms, names, and other details that you need to know. Improvise by

Continued.

FIGURE 4.8

using zany associations within the skit, and act it out to reinforce remembering.

○ If you are having problems remembering terms, names, and other
details when reviewing after class, create memory tools in your
notes, such as mnemonic devices.

○ After class, summarize your notes by creating study cards with
terms/concepts on the front and what they are associated with on
the back.

○ As you review your notes, fill in concrete examples from the text
or lab manual. Add practical applications, effects or outcomes, as
well as personal experiences related to the broader theories.

Examples of students' Personal Action Statements.

FIGURE 4.9

1. I will: _reduce daydreaming during my history class._

2. My greatest hurdle to achieving this is: _I get bored during class._

3. I will eliminate this hurdle by: _(1) participating more during class—_
   asking at least one question each class session; and (2) reviewing
   class material with my classmate Lisa each week.

4. My time frame for achieving this is: _I will begin during tomorrow's class_
   and evaluate when I meet with Lisa each week.

5. My reward for achieving this is: _Feeling like I'm not wasting my time_
   during this class. Also, hopefully I'll be rewarded with a higher
   grade on my next quiz.

1. I will: _highlight important ideas in my philosophy notes after each class._

2. My greatest hurdle to achieving this is: _going back to my room after class_
   to check my e-mail.

3. I will eliminate this hurdle by: _reviewing my notes for 15to20 minutes_
   while I get a cup of coffee and then going back to my room.

4. My time frame for achieving this is: _to begin after my next philosophy_
   class on Wednesday.

5. My reward for achieving this is: _checking my e-mail if I review my_
   notes. I'll see if this motivates me during the next week.

Your Personal Action Statement

1. I will: _____

   _____

   _____

2. My greatest hurdle to achieving this is: _____

   _____

   _____

3. I will eliminate this hurdle by: _____

   _____

   _____

4. My time frame for achieving this is: _____

   _____

   _____

5. My reward for achieving this is: _____

   _____

   _____

Conclusion

As your classes vary, so will your listening and note-taking techniques. New subjects and different instructors will spur you to alter how you best listen, take notes, and study for each course. As you assess and modify strategies, take into account this checklist of basic ingredients for successful and effective class listening and note taking:

Do . . .

- Go to all classes.
- Come rested and fed.
- Bring appropriate supplies: notebook paper and pens/pencils/highlighters or laptop computer.
- Be familiar with the material to be covered in class.
- Sit in front, near the instructor and away from distractions.

- Listen actively; select ideas to write down on notepaper or type on your computer.
- Create notes that are concise, clear, and accurate.
- Be alert; write/type, participate, and consciously *want* to pay attention.
- Adapt to your instructor's style and expectations.
- Review your notes *soon* after class while creating a study guide for yourself.

Don't . . .

- Write/type *every word* your instructor says or *only* words you see on the board.
- Copy classmates' notes or purchase ready-made notes in lieu of taking your own notes.
- Gripe about your instructor and complain about the class. Instead, put your energies toward positive outcomes by obtaining class information, completing assignments, and preparing for tests.

Comprehension Check

The notes in Figure 4.10 are from a class lecture about this chapter. Without looking back through the chapter, use these notes to create an after-class study guide that is complete and accurate. Use at least two of the strategies discussed in this chapter: Fill in incomplete information, add explanations and examples, highlight key words and phrases, summarize key points, and develop questions.

Reference

Pauk, W. (2001). *How to study in college* (7th ed.). Boston: Houghton Mifflin.

FIGURE **4.10**   *Comprehension check.*

	`Date: _____
	CHAP. 4 ACTIVE LISTENING & NOTE TAKING
How alike?	<u>Active listen'g</u> is important because:
	Def. ⟶
How different?	<u>Selective listen'g</u>
	Def. ⟶
	<u>Listening cues</u> are important because:
Describe 2 types of listen'g cues.	<u>Nonverbal cues</u> are:
Give 3 examples of each.	<u>Verbal cues</u> are:

Summary:

CHAPTER 5

Reading and Studying Textbooks

FOCUS QUESTIONS

How can I better *understand* and *remember* what I read?

What are several recommended strategies before, during, and after reading?

Why is each strategy important?

CHAPTER TERMS

After reading the chapter, define (in your own words) and provide an example for each of the following terms:

- close-ended question words
- idea map
- open-ended question words
- previewing
- summary chart
- timeline
- visual study guide

Understanding and Remembering: Five Essential Ingredients

Can you identify with the following student?

Ted has to read Chapter 5 in his *Introduction to Psychology* textbook before tomorrow's class. He opens his text to the beginning of Chapter 5 and then flips to the end to count the pages. To his dismay, the chapter is 30 pages long! He gets out his blue highlighter pen and highlights sentences and paragraphs that, as his eyes move across the page, he thinks are important. He reaches the end of the chapter about an hour later. "Whew, I'm done with that assignment," Ted thinks as he contentedly closes his textbook, expecting to reopen it three weeks from now when he will reread all the blue sections of the pages in preparation for the midterm exam.

However, if someone was to ask Ted to summarize what he just read about in Chapter 5, he could not do it. In fact, the next day in the psychology lecture, Ted was not at all familiar with the terms and ideas that the professor was talking about, even though this material was covered in Chapter 5 of the text. In reality, all Ted accomplished the night before was to create 30 blue pages! He had no understanding, let alone recall, of the important ideas presented in the text chapter.

Ted's method for reading the text material is all too universal. Many students feel a sense of accomplishment with getting the task done, that is, going through the pages, without obtaining a true understanding of what they are reading. If you fall into that category, strategies for reading and studying do exist that can increase both your understanding *and* recall of important information. These strategies are suitable and adaptable for traditional textbooks, novels, and articles as well as electronic books and Web-based reading assignments.

Critical Thinking Task

pause... *and reflect*

Describe yourself as a reader—that is, characterize your usual approach to a reading assignment. Consider these points:

YOUR READING BEHAVIORS: WHAT YOU DO WHEN YOU HAVE AN ASSIGNMENT

- Do you tend to read the assignment immediately or to procrastinate?
- Do you prepare or organize yourself *before* reading? For instance, do you skim through the assignment or look at the end-of-chapter questions or numbers of pages?

- As you read, what do you do? Do you read the whole assignment at one sitting, or do you take frequent breaks? Do you write in your textbook? Do you highlight, take separate notes, or answer study guide questions?
- Are you able to concentrate when reading? How do you keep your mind focused?
- *Afterward*, do you review what you read? Do you reread the entire assignment? Do you quiz yourself?

YOUR ATTITUDE TOWARD READING ASSIGNMENTS

- Are you generally motivated to begin the assignment?
- Do you persist, even if you think the content is boring or difficult to understand?
- Do you often avoid reading? Do you dislike reading? Why?

YOUR LEARNING STYLES, OR PREFERENCES, WHEN READING

- When reading, do you prefer complete silence, or do you prefer music or background noise?
- How long can you read and still maintain your focus: 10 minutes, a half an hour, or how long? How about breaks? Do you need to move around frequently when reading? Do you tend to move your mouth or hear yourself read?
- When reading, do you concentrate best at a particular location and time of day?

You likely will discover that the reading demands for your college courses will be unlike what you have previously encountered. Instructors will expect you to read larger amounts and differing types of materials independently. You will be required to combine reading with class notes, understand complex ideas in print, and analyze multiple sources for discussion and writings. This type of reading, termed *study reading*, demands a high level of comprehension. To be effective, the process you employ for study reading should result in understanding and then recall of important information. The following five steps will guide you toward maximum effectiveness and efficiency in understanding and remembering what you read. Apply these steps when reading hard-copy books and articles, as well as online materials.

1. Preview what's ahead.
2. Break up your reading.
3. Check your understanding.
4. Create study guides.
5. Review periodically.

Preview What's Ahead

Previewing will assist you with learning new, and often complex, information contained in reading assignments. Previewing means getting a quick picture of the whole before proceeding with the detailed parts of a chapter or article. The more familiar you are with any subject or idea, the more likely you will understand it. Familiarize yourself with both the topic and layout of the assignment. The previewing step is a way to build a strong, familiar framework for understanding and remembering new material. In addition, the few minutes you spend previewing can greatly improve your concentration while reading.

GET AN OVERVIEW OF THE BOOK

What parts of a textbook can you glance at to become familiar with the content? The table of contents is important because it presents the overall organization of the book. Also, skim through the preface, introduction, copyright, index, appendixes, and answer keys. You need only do this step once: before you begin reading the first chapter assignment. This quick initial step will provide you with a general idea of the overall layout of the text, the organization of content, the author's viewpoint, and any text-related aids to assist you when reading.

try it out!

Preview a textbook that you are using this term. After previewing, you should be able to answer these questions:

- What are the key components of the text?
- What is the general organization of content?
- How difficult does the text seem to be?
- What related guides, CDs, or Web pages are available?

GET AN OVERVIEW OF THE CHAPTER OR ARTICLE

You want to gain some familiarity with a chapter or article you are about to read. *Previewing* means flipping through pages and glancing at the characteristics of the chapter, including headings, subheadings, introductions, summaries, questions, length, vocabulary/terminology, graphics, spacing, and overall layout. Once you are acquainted with the topics, organization, and difficulty level of the chapter/article, you are prepared to read for both understanding and recall.

try it out!

To understand the benefits of previewing, open your text to a new chapter. Allow yourself *1 minute* to flip through (or scroll down, if using a computer) the pages and note characteristics of the chapter, such as the headings, subheadings, questions, summary, and so on. At the end of a minute, close the text and recite to yourself what you just found out about the chapter. Nothing is too insignificant to note.

You likely will recall information about the chapter's topics and content as well as details about the format, such as the length, graphics, and difficulty level. Most students are surprised about how much information can be gleaned from a chapter in a minute; this information will provide you with a familiar context from which to begin your reading of the assignment.

IDENTIFY YOUR PURPOSE

Why are you reading this chapter? What are you going to do with the information? Your purpose for reading helps you identify how much and what type of information you need to know. If your purpose is to use the information for class discussion, you only need to read to understand the main concepts in the chapter. If your purpose is to do well on the upcoming 100-point test, you will need to read for main ideas as well as for lots of supporting ideas and details. A 10-point quiz on the chapter content means you will need to read primarily for main ideas. Be clear about what type of questions you will be asked and how much detail you are expected to know. Thus, for peak reading efficiency, be clear as to *why* you are reading and *how much* information you need to know.

Break Up Your Reading

For maximum effectiveness, read one section of a chapter or article at a time. Reading a section at a time makes sense because the author has already divided the material into paragraphs around a common topic; therefore, take advantage of these divisions. After reading the section, stop and ask yourself, "What are the key ideas?" If you honestly cannot identify the important ideas, go back and reread the section.

Sometimes reading an entire section at once is too much. If the material is difficult and complicated, you might need to read a paragraph at a time to understand the subject matter fully. Or, if the section is quite long, you may need to divide it up and read several paragraphs before stopping and checking for comprehension. However, do not break up your reading into chunks that are too small. Not only can it become tedious and time consuming to stop after every paragraph, but frequent stops can chop up ideas to the point that the material doesn't flow and, ultimately, doesn't make sense to you.

Check Your Understanding

Critical Thinking Task

Reading is a thought process that involves figuring out what is important, what you need to know, and how you will use the information. Asking questions enhances this thought process by focusing your attention on key ideas and the connections among these ideas. After reading a section, stop and check your understanding by answering questions about the main topic of the passage:

- What are distinguishing characteristics of this topic?
- What are key terms associated with this topic?
- What are significant changes that developed as a result of this topic?
- What are the connections between this and another topic?
- Who are key individuals associated with this topic?
- What conclusions can I draw about this topic?
- What's important for me to know about this topic?
- How will I use information about this topic for this course?
- What confuses me about this topic?

Reading to discover the answers to these and similar questions focuses your attention, promotes thinking, and ultimately helps you develop meaning out of the written text. To maximize your comprehension of the passage, answer the questions in your own words.

Create Study Guides

Combining reading with studying is an effective and efficient technique. Unlike Ted, described at the beginning of this chapter, do not separate the two. As you check your understanding of the passage, write down or highlight points to remember.

- Answer questions.
- Paraphrase, in your own words, key ideas.
- Add details and explanations.
- Provide concrete examples and meaningful situations.

By writing down or highlighting important points, you will be (1) immediately reinforcing the information, and (2) developing a study guide for later review.

You have choices as to the type of study guide you can create. Your decision depends on your purpose for reading, your background and familiarity with the subject, the difficulty level of the text, your learning preferences, and what you need to know for the upcoming quiz, exam, or discussion. The purpose of a study guide is to help you select, organize, understand, and remember key information for your course.

An effective study guide presents information in an organized, concise manner and helps you learn and recall text information. The intent of a study guide is to maximize both the effectiveness and the efficiency by which you study for your courses. Types of study guides that are useful for college students are described on the following pages.

QUESTION-AND-ANSWER STUDY GUIDE

Three words that are key to increasing your reading comprehension and concentration are *what*, *why*, and *how*. These are termed **open-ended question words** because they generate answers that are broader and more conceptual than do the other three question words: *who*, *when*, and *where*. The answers to what, why, and how tend to be *main ideas*. The answers to who, when, and where, in contrast, tend to be *specific facts*, which is the reason they are termed **close-ended question words.**

For the question-and-answer study guide, you develop questions to guide your reading; that is, you read to discover the answers to questions. If the chapter or article that you are reading contains headings, use the headings as a basis for creating questions. Otherwise, create your own questions. To focus on main ideas and concepts, use what, why, and how questions. If you need to know details for tests, add who, when, and where questions. After reading a section, think about—and write or type—the answer to each question. Write your question and accompanying answer in the textbook, on a separate sheet of paper, on index cards, or type on the computer for later self-testing.

Figure 5.1 provides an example of study guide questions created from chapter headings. By creating questions and then answering the questions, you will be actively identifying important ideas within a section and thus becoming a more focused reader. In addition, you will have developed a question-and-answer study guide for later review.

Example of study guide questions.   FIGURE **5.1**

1. heading: The Steps of the Scientific Method
   question: What are the steps of the scientific method?

2. heading: Forming a Hypothesis
   question: How should I form a hypothesis?

3. heading: The Importance of Observation
   question: Why is observation an important part of the scientific method?

4. heading: The Baroque Era of Music
   questions: What are the major characteristics of baroque music?
               Who were the major composers during the era?
               When did the baroque period begin and end?

"I used to just jump in and read. Now, I begin by reading the introduction and conclusion; this gives me a general idea of what I will be reading. Also, I change headings into questions and try to answer those questions to see how much I comprehend. These are the best habits that I've gotten into." —SHI-ANN

"When I have a chapter to read, the first thing I do is turn all headings and subheadings into questions. I also look for italicized and boldfaced words and turn them into questions. I then skim through the section, looking for the answer. This greatly cuts down on both the time it takes me to read and unnecessary note taking." —DENNIS

HIGHLIGHTING-PLUS-MARKING STUDY GUIDE

The advantage of highlighting and underlining is that you can emphasize important ideas in the text without rewriting the ideas on a separate sheet of paper. Consider these factors when highlighting.

1. **Read first and then highlight.** If you highlight *as* you read, it is difficult to distinguish important from unimportant ideas. Also, because ideas are often repeated within a section, you tend to overhighlight if you don't read the material first. In addition, highlighting while you read can disrupt concentration. Instead, read the section first, and then use highlighting as a means to check your understanding of key ideas. For online reading, use the highlighting function of the word processing program or the writing function if using a tablet PC.

2. **Highlight as little as possible to get the idea across.** Most students err on the side of overhighlighting—that is, they think nearly everything is important. This defeats the purpose of a study guide; if you emphasize too much, you end up rereading most of the chapter or article. Instead, focus on key words or phrases that get the idea across. Avoid highlighting whole sentences or, worse yet, whole paragraphs. If everything in a paragraph is noteworthy, use markings to emphasize *what* and *why* the information is important.

The advantage of adding markings on a page is that you are not limited to just the words used in the text. Markings help make important ideas clearer and more distinct. Such markings include:

- *Summarizing* a passage with a short phrase [e.g., "visual learn'g preferences"].
- Indicating the *organization* of material [e.g., (1) (2) (3)].
- Using *symbols* to *emphasize* ideas [e.g., +, >, $\longrightarrow$, *].
- Indicating *why ideas are important to know* [e.g., "How am I a visual learner?"].

Example of highlighting plus marking.   FIGURE **5.2**

---

visual learn'g preferences

Bio. Prof.
Dr. Ada Worth is a visual learner and, therefore, relies on visual strategies and
3 ex. of tchng. strategies
materials when teaching her biology classes. For lectures, she writes most of the
(1)   *(2)*
ideas on the board and often uses the overhead projector. Also, she gives students
(3)   *3 ex. of student expectations*
handouts illustrating material covered in each class. Furthermore, she wants
(1)
students to use the mapping format of note taking to summarize articles discussed
(2)
in class. Finally, she expects students to keep their lab areas free of clutter and to
(3)
write neat, clear notes in their lab manuals.

* How am I a visual lrner??

Markings combined with highlighting or underlining is an effective study guide because you are *interacting* with the text material, making ideas as explicit as possible. Figure 5.2 provides an example of a highlighting-plus-marking study guide.

OUTLINING STUDY GUIDE

You likely are familiar with the standard format for outlining a passage: organizing notes by writing main ideas to the left with supporting ideas underneath, indenting to the right as ideas become less general and more detailed. Outlining is most effective if you paraphrase ideas presented in the text, that is, if you write—or type—key points in *your own words*, adding explanations or examples. In Figure 5.3, note the use of action words to begin the phrases in the outline.

STUDY CARDS

Study cards are especially effective when you need to know terms and definitions, including examples and applications of the term. The front of an index

"I *never* marked books—it was not allowed. Even today, if I make a stray mark or accidentally bend a page, I am appalled at my own carelessness! I recently realized that my attitude needs to change if I am to survive as a college student; I am learning to value books in a different way. Lately, I've been underlining important ideas, and so far the book hasn't self-destructed!" **—NICOLE**

"In the past, textbook reading seemed a waste of time. I would think, "Why read the textbook when the professor gives us notes?" However, it was impossible for me to excel this way, so I started reading and highlighting. At first I was highlighting *everything* in the chapter. I was reading chapters two or three times because I thought everything was important, which is why I got bored when reading. Since then, I have highlighted *words*, not entire sentences. This has helped me to slow down and understand more precisely what I am reading. Also, I discovered that marking in the margins makes the important points stand out so that they catch my eye." **—GAVIN**

"Often, the class material and book material are parallel. Thus I read the chapter *before* class so that I can more easily keep up with the instructor's lecture. I bring my book notes to class and mark in the margins what the instructor goes over so I know what to study for a test. I always mark examples used in class; examples make great memory joggers in the middle of a 'blank out' during a test. In addition, if I have a question in class, I see if I can answer it myself by first referring to my book notes." **—KATE**

"I hate to read; it bores me. Having said this, I prefer to use my laptop computer and make an outline as I read each section. I then study my outline and class lecture notes to acquire the necessary knowledge." **—TODD**

card showcases a name, term, concept, or main idea. Putting the term or idea in a question format helps you focus on what you need to know. For instance, if you are reading about the scientific method, on the front of your study card write, "What are steps of the scientific method?" On the back, write the

Example of outlining.   FIGURE **5.3**

Dr. Ada Worth is a visual learner and, therefore, relies on visual strategies and materials when teaching her biology classes. For lectures, she writes most of the ideas on the board and often uses the overhead projector. Also, she gives students handouts illustrating material covered in each class. She wants students to use the mapping format of note taking to summarize articles discussed in class. Finally, she expects students to keep their lab areas free of clutter and to write neat, clear notes in their lab manuals.

I. Dr. Worth ⟶ visual lrnr./instructor
   A. Lecture techniques
      1. Writes on board
      2. Uses overhead projector
   B. Provides handouts
   C. Uses mapping
   D. Lab expectations
      1. Neat environment
      2. Neat student notes

definition, explanation, example, or other appropriate details. Be concise and use your own words.

An advantage of study cards is that you must be *selective* when reading a text because you are separating text information into individual parts for the front and back of the cards. Study cards can help you pinpoint main ideas and related details in the text. In addition, study cards are excellent tools for quizzing yourself orally and teaching others. Create study cards if you want *repetitive* reinforcement of text information.

However, a disadvantage of study cards is the tendency for students to memorize, as opposed to learn, the information. Study cards generally are not effective for in-depth analysis and synthesis of text material. Figure 5.4 shows two examples of study cards.

FIGURE **5.4**   *Examples of study cards.*

FRONTS

What are <u>sedimentary</u> rocks?

Why important?

What are <u>metamorphic</u> rocks?

Why important?

BACKS

— Made of particles;
fragments cemented together.

— Gives clues to ancient
environment & climates.

— Any igneous or sed. rock
that is burned; changes form.

— Gives clues about plate
tectonics.

VISUAL STUDY GUIDES: MAPS, CHARTS, AND TIMELINES

Most people learn and recall best when they can visualize information. Idea maps, summary charts, and timelines are all visual summaries of ideas in print. A **visual study guide** involves *active reading* of text material to

1. Identify key ideas—both major and minor—in the text passage.
2. Identify relationships among these ideas.
3. Create an organized, concise summary.

Reading to fill in a map, chart, or timeline can be an efficient method of reading a text. First, identify the overall relationships among ideas in the passage and create a frame for your chart or map. By first recognizing the categories or type of information you need to know, you will be eliminating unneeded information when reading the text. Then read to complete the study guide. This technique of reading to fill in a chart, map, or timeline can speed up your reading and thus is an efficient reading strategy.

Furthermore, visual guides are excellent tools to use for review before exams. To create a visual study guide, you will be organizing, categorizing, and simplifying text information, all of which result in *knowing* the material. The concise visual image provides a perfect format for speedy overviews before a test. A number of computer programs are available that enable you to create a variety of visual study guides.

Models of visual study guides include the following:

- **Idea maps** (Figure 5.5) are especially appropriate for showing the connections among main ideas and subordinate supporting ideas.
- **Summary charts** (Figure 5.6) present an effective framework for summarizing and categorizing key features, including definitions, characteristics, accompanying examples, and relationships.
- **Timelines** (Figure 5.7) are suitable for material organized in chronological order, such as a progression of events or steps in a process.

Four examples of idea maps.   FIGURE **5.5**

I. The **topic** (*1960s Protest Movements*) is divided into *three* **main ideas** each of which has offshoots—**supporting ideas** with **details**. Note the parallel placement of the supporting ideas with similar themes: 1) which phase of the movement, and 2) people.

Protest Movements of the 1960s

Civil Rights	Women's Rights	Vietnam War
later phase of movement	early phase of movement	height of movement
based on civil disobedience, but violence increases	offshoot of civil rights movement	youth rebel against establishment
Black Panthers		protest war
		draft dodging
Martin Luther King Jr.	Betty Friedan	Chicago Seven
I Have a Dream speech	The Feminine Mystique	violence–Democratic
Nobel Peace Prize	N.O.W.	National Convention
assassinated in 1968		

(continued)

FIGURE **5.5** *Continued.*

II. The **topic** (*"STUDY CARDS for reading"*) is divided into two distinct **categories** (*"ADVANTAGES"* & *"DISADVANTAGES"*):

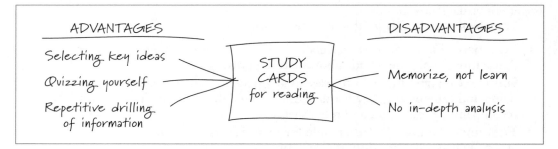

III. This idea map presents the two parts ("active" vs. "inactive") related to the topic ("quiet breathing"):

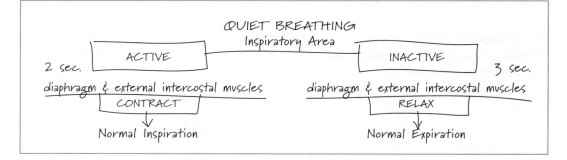

IV. This idea map illustrates a **cause-and-effect** relationship among ideas. The topic is "THE INDUSTRIAL REVOLUTION":

The 1769 invention of the steam engine by J. Watt in Great Britain
resulted in ↳Saved fuel costs
  ↳Growth in machinery used in mines, mills, railroads, ships
    ↳Technologies spread to continental Europe & "New World"
      ↳Increased quality and affordability of products
        ↳Expanding prosperity
          ↳Increased health, education, leisure, and mobility
            ↳Growth of middle class
              ↳Increased expectations for future generation
                ↳an Industrial Boom!

Two examples of summary charts.   FIGURE 5.6

PSYCHOLOGICAL DISORDERS

TYPES	DEFINITION	EXAMPLES	FEELINGS
<u>Anxiety</u>	Characterized by distressing, persistent anxiety	1) Panic attacks—last several minutes; intense dread 2) Phobias—fears	Chest pain, choking, smothering sensation, rapid heartbeat
<u>Somatoform</u>	Symptoms take solo form w/ no physical cause	1) Conversion disorder— anxiety is converted into physical symptoms 2) Hypochondria—interrupts normal sensations	Dizziness, vomiting, blurred vision
<u>Dissociative</u>	Conscious awareness becomes separated from memories	1) Amnesia—failure to recall events 2) Fugue—fleeing one's home & identity for days/months	Facing trauma, forgot what was intolerable, painful, the way they should act or feel
<u>Mood</u>	Emotional extremes	1) Major depression— prolonged depression 2) Bipolar disorder— alternates between depression and mania	Lack of energy, not able to eat/sleep normally, better off dead; much pressure

FIGURE **5.6** *Continued.*

Cause-and-Effect Chart for Civil Rights Movement

CAUSE	EFFECT
Southern closed society	- Blacks excluded from politics - Whites controlled economy - Segregation is the norm
13th Amendment	- Ends slavery
14th Amendment	- Nobody can be processed without due process
15th Amendment	- Black men allowed to vote
Jim Crow laws	- Revokes blacks of all their rights
Plessy v. Ferguson 1896	- Establishes doctrine "separate but equal"
Black soldiers returning from WWII	- Demanded jobs (learned skills during war) and desegregation
Brown v. Board of Education (1954)	- Most important civil rights case - Ruled unanimously that "separate but equal" is not equal
Southern manifesto	- 100 congressmen oppose desegregation - Say it violates the Constitution and the 14th Amendment
Montgomery bus boycott	- Strong black community - MLK Jr. put into national role - Combination of legal strategies and nonviolent direct action - Protest begins the movement - SCLC is formed

[Created by Melissa Swope]

Two examples of timelines.   FIGURE **5.7**

Feminist Movement

Time Period: Goals, Accomplishments, & Characteristics:

| 1st Wave | 1848–1950's |

1. 1848: Start of Women's suffrage movement. Delegates to Women's Rights Convention, Seneca Falls, NY, adopted Declaration of Sentiments. 1st public demand for women's independ. Supporters insulted, assaulted, &/or ignored by pop. press & leaders.
2. 1900: Suffragists publicly marched protesting for right to vote.
3. 1920: Women received right to vote.
4. Break from women's traditional roles of dependency & submission.

| 2nd Wave | 1960s–1980s |

1. Women's continuing social, legal, & financial independence & self-direction.
2. Enlightenment of options in & out of home.
3. "Equal Pay for Equal Work."
4. Opening doors in nontraditional workplaces.
5. Reproductive choices & freedoms.
6. Primarily involved white middle-class women.

| 3rd Wave | 1990s–21st Century |

1. Breaking the so-called glass ceiling to top positions within workplaces.
2. Addressing race & class inequalities.
3. Overcoming domestic violence & rape.
4. Rights of homosexuals & transgendered people.
5. Broadening scope of feminism.
6. Focus feminism on daily practicality, as opposed to theory & intellectuality.

(continued)

FIGURE **5.7** *Continued.*

U.S. Involvement in Vietnam War

Nixon vs. Humphrey
presidential elections

1st U.S. advisers   Nixon wins—   U.S. embassy
sent to   LBJ sends 1st U.S.   promises   U.S. troops   evacuated.
S. Vietnam   combat troops   to end war   withdraw   Saigon falls

        1955   1965   1968   1971   1975

1945   1960   1966   1969   1973

Democrat Republic   JFK plans to   385,000   542,000   50,000
of Vietnam—   withdraw.   U.S. troops. U.S. troops.   U.S. troops.

Ho Chi Minh   NLF formed   War becomes   Armistice
proclaims   U.S. sends   increasingly less signed.
independence.   2,000 "advisers."   winnable for U.S.

Review Periodically

t least once a week, look over your study guide. This regular review keeps the many and varied pieces of information rooted in your memory. Here are some approaches for weekly review.

ADD OR COMBINE LECTURE MATERIAL

Are there parts of the text that help clarify complex ideas from the lecture or vice versa? Can you identify overlapping text and lecture information, information that likely will be on a future exam? Can you see how parts of the text and lecture relate to one another and combine to form an image of the whole?

TALK ALOUD

As you review, say the information aloud, either to yourself or to another person. Use as many of your senses as possible to learn and remember the new information—*see* the information in your study guide, *say* the information aloud, and *hear* yourself, thus reinforcing the subject matter. If possible, teach someone else as you review; find a friend, classmate, or family member who will listen and ask questions as you explain the information. If you are able to clearly *teach* it to another person, you likely *know* it.

ANTICIPATE TEST QUESTIONS

Predict and write down questions you expect to appear on the upcoming quiz or exam. This tactic will help you be selective with quantities of information. Also, you will be thinking of the information in terms of immediate use, that is, knowing it for the test.

Here are the steps for reading an assignment effectively and efficiently:

1. Preview to obtain a general idea of what's ahead.
2. Read a section.

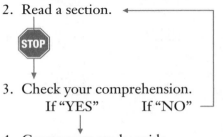

3. Check your comprehension.
    If "YES"   If "NO"
4. Create your study guide.
5. Review periodically to help you remember.

try it out!

Critical Thinking Task

Using your current course assignments, create and use the various types of study guides. After using each study guide, **Assess Your Success** by writing its advantages and disadvantages on Figure 5.8. Use the following four questions to guide you as you judge the value and drawbacks of each type of study guide:

1. Does this study guide assist me to *understand* the content as I read?
2. Does this study guide help keep my attention *focused* on what I am reading?
3. Does this study guide assist me to *remember* important information?
4. Is this study guide a worthwhile tool for *review* before a test?

FIGURE **5.8**   *Assessing study guides.*

Study Guide	Advantages	Disadvantages
Question and Answer		
Highlighting plus Marking		
Outlining		
Study Cards		
Idea Map		
Summary Chart		
Timeline		

try it out!

Learning Style and Reading/Studying Strategies

Critical Thinking Task

Figure 5.9 links learning styles with reading strategies. You will select, implement, and assess a specific strategy that matches your learning preference.

1. Using Figure 5.9, in the right column circle your dominant learning preference—*visual, aural, read/write,* or *kinesthetic.* If you are multidimensional, that is, dominant in more than one modality, circle all that apply.

2. Refer to the reading and studying strategies beside each of your preferences and place a check in the circles next to those that you do use regularly.

3. Identify one strategy that would help you when you read and study. Write a Personal Action Statement showing how you will apply that strategy when reading your next assignment.

4. After completing the strategy, refer back to your Personal Action Statement and **Assess Your Success:**
   - Did you accomplish what you set out to do? Explain.
   - Describe how you were able to overcome any obstacles.

- Think about your experience and how successful you were with understanding and remembering what you read. What additional behaviors or different techniques can you implement to make your system of reading and study effective and efficient for *you*? Incorporate these new strategies in a Personal Action Statement for your next reading assignment.

Reading and studying strategies and learning preferences FIGURE **5.9**

READING AND STUDYING STRATEGIES	LEARNING PREFERENCES
○ To help your comprehension, get an overview *before* reading. Look at the introduction, headings, and summary.	
○ When reading, *focus on main ideas first* (look at the first and last sentences; read the summary) to understand the big picture. Then, go back and read more carefully for details.	
○ When reading, focus on seeing relationships or organization of ideas. Use symbols such as arrows and marginal notations that show the relationships of ideas within a passage.	
○ For longer passages, break up your reading by using highlighters and colored pens for visual emphasis. Use color-coded tabs to separate topics and chapters.	**Visual**
○ Create visual study guides: Organize text information by creating an *idea map* relating main ideas with details. Or develop a *chart* that illustrates key names/terms and accompanying characteristics or details. Or develop a *timeline* of key events.	
○ Color-code your highlighting according to type of content. For example, green for important terms, pink for important people, blue if the information was reviewed in class, and yellow for general knowledge. This can be especially useful for social science textbooks.	
○ For terms, make colorful study cards with the term on the front and a brief explanation on the back.	
○ Especially for complex and important information, heighten your comprehension by talking aloud as you read so that you hear yourself.	
○ Class lectures and discussion are often your strength, so use class information as a basis for understanding the text. Review lecture notes before reading. Keep notes handy as you read, thinking about how class information fits into text readings.	**Aural**
○ Use books on tape, following along as your read. Or create a tape of yourself reading out loud.	

(continued)

FIGURE **5.9**   *Continued.*

○ Participate in group study and review sessions to *discuss* text information. Compare and contrast your study guides with others.

○ Teach others; this will reinforce what you *know* about subjects.

○ Use supplemental materials on companion Websites or CDs that provide auditory reinforcement.

○ Reading often is a strength for you. Read or skim through text material before class, using your reading as a basis for understanding what you hear in lectures.

○ For illustrations and other graphic materials, write out details that explain the information.

○ Your preferences are an advantage in developing a thorough text study guide by highlighting plus marking.

○ Develop a study guide by writing or typing an outline that summarizes important text information.

Read/write

○ Text reading is often your weakness. Thus use a simple question-and-answer (*what, how, why, who, when, where*) study guide for text reading. This will expedite your reading while focusing your attention on important ideas.

○ *If you prefer variety and action, speed up your reading:* **(1)** focus on the first and last sentences of paragraphs; **(2)** use chapter headings as guides to identify main ideas; **(3)** create a study guide by turning headings into questions, then read to answer the questions.

○ Move your fingers across the page as you read.

○ Pace around the room as you read, or act out what you are reading.

○ Make associations between new information and real-life experiences—as you read jot down the associations. Use lab and field work as a means to strengthen your understanding of written material.

○ Read for short chunks of time, taking regular breaks where you move about.

○ Use supplemental materials on companion Websites or CDs that provide animated three-dimensional experiments and demonstrations.

Kinesthetic

Conclusion

BEFORE YOU READ

- **Know why you are reading the material.** What are you going to do with the information? Are you taking a short quiz, a longer exam, or an essay test, or is this information for class discussion? Tailor your reading to fit the purpose of each assignment.

- **Get an overview of the chapter or article.**
  - Skim over headings, italicized and boldfaced print, the introduction, the summary, and the questions at the end.
  - Note the order and difficulty level of material.
  - Anticipate how long you will need to read for an understanding of the information.

DURING YOUR READING

- **Break up your reading.** Reading in small chunks of time helps keep your concentration high and your mind focused.
- **Think about what is important to know.** If you read to discover ideas, you will increase your understanding of the material.
- **Create a study guide.** This should reflect what you need to know for the upcoming exam or discussion.

"Surveying helps me see what the author is trying to teach. I make my own questions and try to answer them; this helps keep me interested in the reading. Reciting my answers helps me know if I really understand what I am reading. Constant review has saved me from forgetting (which I'm a real expert at doing). Reviewing keeps the subject fresh and pulls the main ideas together to give an overview of what the author is expressing." —PATRICE

STUDENT VOICES

AFTER YOU READ

- *Review* your study guides weekly.
  - Review the text with the lecture.
  - Talk aloud.
  - Anticipate test questions.

See Figure 5.10 for a summary of study guides.

Comprehension Check

Return to the focus questions on page 75. Jot down an answer for each question as if you were creating a question-and-answer study guide. Or answer the questions as an outlining study guide.

For each chapter term make a study card; write the term on the front and your definition and example on the back. Or, complete a three-column summary chart with these three headings: Term, Definition, and Example.

Your Personal Action Statement

Identify a reading assignment:

1. I will: _____
   _____
   _____

2. My greatest hurdle to achieving this is: _____
   _____
   _____

3. I will eliminate this hurdle by: _____
   _____
   _____

4. My time plan for achieving this is: _____
   _____
   _____

5. My reward for achieving this is: _____
   _____
   _____

Summary of study guides.   **FIGURE 5.10**

Description	Advantages	Disadvantages
QUESTIONS AND ANSWERS		
Develop questions from headings/subheadings; Then *read to discover the answers.*	• Predicting questions will increase your reading comprehension. • *What, why, how* questions direct your attention to *key ideas,* thus increasing concentration while reading. • You tend to read faster; thus is beneficial for a *large amount* of reading.	• By reading *just* to answer a question, you could be missing other key ideas. • Not effective when careful, detailed reading is necessary.
HIGHLIGHTING *PLUS* MARKING		
After reading a section, *highlight words* or *phrases* representing key ideas. *Add markings* to summarize, organize, and/or emphasize important information.	• Beneficial if you need to know *much text information,* that is, main ideas *plus* details. • An effective and convenient method of *emphasizing ideas* right on the page.	• Effectiveness is greatly reduced if you highlight *too much* or *too little* or if you don't add markings. • Can consume more time than other types of study guides.
OUTLINING		
Write key points in your own words; indent for progressive details. Add explanations or examples.	• Effective if you prefer to *rewrite information* for maximum recall. • Worthwhile if you prefer to learn material in a *linear format.*	• By just rewriting boldfaced headings and subheadings, you will create an easy, but *ineffective,* study guide.
STUDY CARDS		
On front, write question, term, concept, or main idea. *On back,* write definition, explanation, example, or supporting details.	• Especially effective for recall of *terms and definitions.* • Separates information into individual parts. • An easy format for oral quizzes.	• Tendency to *memorize* as opposed to *learning* new info. • Difficult to show effectively how ideas are related or organized.
VISUAL GUIDES—*Maps, Charts, Timelines*		
A concise summary that indicates how ideas are organized or related. A variety of formats: chart, idea map, or timeline.	• Forms a *visual* picture of written material, which increases recall. • An *efficient* way to read: when you "fill in" the frame of the chart or map you created, you eliminate unneeded information.	• Can be difficult or confusing, especially if you are unused to identifying relationships among ideas. • Limits the amount of details that can be included.

C H A P T E R 6

Enhancing Your Memory

FOCUS QUESTIONS

Describe the six memory-enhancing techniques presented in this chapter.

How are sleep, time management, and memory connected?

Describe a situation in which you used your senses to enhance your memory.

CHAPTER TERMS

After reading the chapter, define (in your own words) and provide an example for each of the following terms:

- association
- mnemonic device
- visualization

ESSENTIAL INGREDIENTS

College Studying

Memory: Six Essential Ingredients

egrettably, a magical formula to boost one's memory does not exist. It is the commonsense study habits and strategies, implemented consistently, that strengthen memory. Many of these strategies were described in Chapters 2 through 5. This chapter highlights six fundamental ingredients to enhance learning and improve memory:

1. Get enough sleep.
2. Study in small, regular blocks of time.
3. Review soon after receiving new information.
4. Organize and categorize information.
5. Use your senses.
6. Associate ideas.

Get Enough Sleep

egular, adequate nighttime sleep is a critical element of the memory process. For college students, insufficient sleep is a major reason for poor recall. Research studies confirm the far-reaching and damaging effect that lack of sleep has on performance and memory. Therefore, by maintaining 8 to 10 hours of uninterrupted sleep nightly, you will greatly enhance your thinking ability, including recall of information.

In addition, daytime naps, usually lasting no more than 60 minutes, can benefit your academic performance. Research studies using magnetic resonance imaging (MRI) scans of the brain demonstrate how midday naps can improve brain functioning and revive mental alertness, as illustrated by Eve's experience (see nearby "Student Voices").

"Three or four days a week, I take what I refer to as a *power nap*. A power nap is lying down and sleeping for an hour in the afternoon. If I sleep more than one hour, I wake up feeling tired, not refreshed. Since I work until 2 A.M. some mornings and never get the same amount of sleep every night, these power naps are important to me." —EVE

STUDENT VOICES

The bottom line is that a well-rested student understands and remembers more and therefore performs better than the sleep-deprived student.

Study in Small, Regular Blocks of Time

Your memory will be clearer at the beginning and at the end of any task or situation; it is the middle section that often becomes muddled and less clear. For instance, you likely remember the beginning stage of high school when you were a new freshman going into an unfamiliar building, meeting new teachers, having new challenges, and so forth. In addition, the last part of your high school experiences—your senior year—likely provides memorable impressions in your mind. The middle years tend to be less distinct and more tangled.

Also consider the amount of time for study sessions. Most people lose their mental energy and concentration after 30 to 60 minutes; thus plan accordingly. You can increase your mental recall by simply dividing one long study session into shorter sessions of no more than an hour. Take a short break between sessions by switching activities. This change of activities provides your brain with time to rest and to process the information that, in turn, strengthens your recollection. (*Note:* This strategy also applies when scheduling classes: You likely will learn and remember more in three 1-hour class sessions per week as opposed to one 3-hour class session.)

Therefore, a method of increasing your memory is to study information in small blocks of time with a short break between sessions. The blocks of study time that you set aside for an assignment depends on certain factors:

- **Subject Matter.** Most students are able to concentrate for longer periods of time when working with material they find interesting or relevant.
- **Difficulty Level.** Most students are able to concentrate for longer periods of time when the information is not so difficult as to cause frustration nor so easy as to cause boredom.
- **Time of Day.** Students stay focused longer when they are feeling fresh and alert.

Plan ahead and consider the factors just listed when scheduling blocks of time for study and review.

Review Soon After Receiving New Information

Repetition embeds information in the mind and therefore is key to memory. Begin reviewing *soon* after your initial exposure to the information so you don't have to relearn the subject matter.

"I found out that most people retain only about 20% of what they supposedly learned during the day. Therefore, rereading my class notes at night has been a good idea; it works as a reinforcement. I also review my textbook material more frequently. This has made test preparation go a lot easier and quicker for me. Plus, there are fewer things on the test that do not look familiar." **—BEN**

Organize and Categorize Information

The more you can establish relationships among ideas, the more you tend to remember the ideas. Linking or grouping information will enhance your recall of the subject matter. For example, a student studying for an upcoming quiz in a biology class created the summary chart in Figure 6.1. Note the three distinct categories and four parallel phases under each category. This student created an organized framework by which to remember key information.

Critical thinking task

Use Your Senses

Review information regularly, using as many of your senses and modalities as possible. The more hands-on multisensory activities you employ, the more likely you are to retain the information.

Example of organizing and categorizing.   FIGURE **6.1**

MITOSIS	MEIOSIS I	MEIOSIS II
Prophase:	Prophase I:	Prophase II:
Metaphase:	Metaphase I:	Metaphase II:
Anaphase:	Anaphase I:	Anaphase II:
Telophase:	Telophase I:	Telophase II:

FIGURE **6.2** *Example of visualization.*

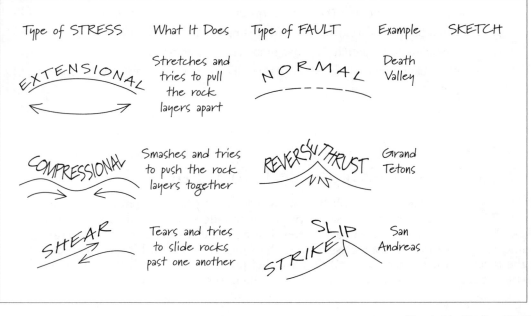

[Created by Heather Kline]

"I feel that if I write something out on paper, I am more likely to remember it than if I just underline or highlight. For example, in choosing a textbook study guide, I prefer to write down important ideas in my notebook next to the class notes referring to the same topic. If needed, I will draw pictures or diagrams from the book into my notes. By integrating a text chapter with class notes, I am able to see the whole picture at once. Currently, I am enjoying the feeling of really *knowing* the material." **—NIKITA**

- **Seeing.** Create visual pictures, and illustrate and color-code ideas. **Visualization,** forming a mental picture, is a vital component of memory. By visualizing information, you will be implanting images in your mind and thus retaining more. For instance, for a geoscience course, a student created an organized framework with several visual emphases; she added gradients and differences in lettering as well as a column to sketch each type of stress/fault (see Figure 6.2).

- **Saying.** Talk to yourself or to others. Join a study group to discuss and teach one another the subject matter.
- **Hearing.** Recite aloud to hear the information. Again, studying with others will provide opportunities to listen to people talking about the subject matter.
- **Touching.** Use your sense of touch to emphasize shapes, textures, and contours of materials. For example, for a geology course, try feeling different types of rocks or tracing the outlines of geological formations.
- **Doing.** Write down information, act out scenarios, play a game, or simply move about while reciting information. For example, students in a study group for a general psychology course played charades when trying to remember psychological disorders. They acted out the various types of disorders while others guessed the name of the disorder and corresponding treatment. Reviewing information using a similar action game can make a profound and lasting impact on your memory.

Critical
Thinking
Task

pause... *and reflect*

The first five ingredients for enhancing memory—(1) get adequate sleep; (2) study in small, regular blocks of time; (3) review soon after receiving new information; (4) organize and categorize; and (5) use your senses—were presented in previous chapters.

1. Refer to Chapter 2, "Managing Your Time," and reconsider the elements of sleep and regular blocks of study time.
   - To improve your memory skills, where should you make changes?
   - Do you need to increase sleep by going to bed earlier or inserting power naps?

2. Refer to Chapter 4, "Active Listening and Note Taking," and reevaluate your habits.
   - Should you add review time soon after certain classes to improve your learning?
   - What do you do with your lecture notes to enhance your understanding and, ultimately, recall of important information?
   - Do you need to create more or different study guides for lecture notes to improve your memory of key information?

3. Refer to the "Visual Study Guides: Maps, Charts, and Timelines" section of Chapter 5, "Reading and Studying Textbooks" (p. 86). Development of a visual study guide involves identifying and organizing key ideas within a visual format; thus maps, summary charts, and timelines often enhance retention.

- How often do you create and use visual study guides when reading?
- How about when preparing for an exam? Have you developed a study guide that summarizes course material in a concise visual format?
- Describe a map, chart, or timeline that was effective in improving your recall in a particular subject.

Associate Ideas

Association means relating or linking new information to that with which you already know. By connecting *new* ideas with familiar ideas already rooted in your mind, you can form memorable images to boost immediate recall. Be inventive and unique when linking ideas together; silly, exaggerated, or bizarre associations will produce lasting remembrances.

Association is best employed for short-term recall of facts and details that you tend to forget because the information is complex, unfamiliar, meaningless, or without context. For example, a student in a chemistry course created the following association to help her remember the details of the structure of the atom:

> "Visualize an **atom** as an *apartment building*: an atom has many different **shells** and an apartment building has many different *floors*. Each shell has **subshells**, and each floor holds *apartments* of differing sizes. The apartments are collections of *rooms*, and the subshells are collections of **orbitals**."
>
> —Carly M. Solazzo

Critical Thinking Task

pause... *and reflect*

Mnemonic devices are another type of memory tool best used for short-term recall of details. An effective mnemonic device is simple to devise and easy to remember. The disadvantages of mnemonic devices include the following:

1. You are *remembering*, not *learning*, information.
2. They can be cumbersome to create and easily confused when you most want to remember details accurately and clearly, that is, when taking the test!

EXAMPLES OF MNEMONIC DEVICES

1. Creating a catchy rhyme, jingle, or song:
   - Remembering specific biology researchers and types of cells each studied: "People go slipping and **Schliden** on **Plant** cells and **Schwann** (swan) for **Animal** cells."

- Remembering number of days for each month: "Thirty days has September, April, June, and November; all the rest have 31, except February, which has 28."
2. Using the first letter of words to develop a word or phrase:
   - A campus building: *Hadley Union Building* = "HUB"
   - Piaget's Stages of Cognitive Development:
   <u>S</u>heila (Sensorimotor)
   and
   <u>P</u>eter (Preoperational)
   <u>C</u>ounted (Concrete operational)
   <u>F</u>rogs (Formal operational)

When have you used mnemonic devices to remember details? Describe several situations to share with classmates.

try it out

Learning Style and Memory Strategies

Figure 6.3 links learning styles with memory strategies. You will select, implement, and assess a specific strategy that matches your learning preference.

1. Using Figure 6.3, in the right column circle your dominant learning preference—*visual, aural, read/write, or kinesthetic*. If you are multidimensional, that is, dominant in more than one modality, circle all that apply.
2. Refer to the memory strategies beside each of your preferences and place a check in the boxes next to those that you do use regularly.
3. Identify one strategy that would help enhance your memory. Write a Personal Action Statement showing how you will apply the strategy in a course this week.
4. After completing the strategy, refer back to your Personal Action Statement and **Assess Your Success:**
   - Did you accomplish what you set out to do? Explain.
   - Describe how you were able to overcome any obstacles.
   - Think about your experience and how successful you were with remembering. What additional behaviors or different techniques can you implement?

Critical Thinking Task

FIGURE **6.3**   *Memory strategies and learning preferences.*

MEMORY STRATEGIES	LEARNING PREFERENCES

○ Visualize information in your mind. Strengthen your recall by imagining that you see the information.

○ Make color-coded study cards, especially for terms. Use symbols and illustrations to help you visualize the information.

Visual

○ Use sticky notes as visual reminders. Place the notes in accessible locations, such as on your computer, a bathroom mirror, refrigerator, or front door.

○ To remember steps for a problem or process, such as with math and science course work, develop a flowchart or diagram that separates each step.

○ Recite aloud while reviewing.

○ Talk and interact with others to improve memory.

○ Create a catchy rhyme, jingle, or song as a memory technique.

Aural

○ To remember steps for a problem or process, such as with math and science course work, talk out loud as you move through each step.

○ To strengthen recall, imagine hearing the information.

○ Rewrite as a method of review.

○ Separate and write out details of each step for a problem or process, such as with math and science course work.

Read/write

○ Create mnemonic devices by using the first letter of words to develop a new word or phrase.

○ To strengthen memory, use all of your senses—sight, touch, taste, smell, and hearing.

○ Move about and read aloud while reviewing.

○ Whenever possible create three-dimensional models of information.

○ Act out roles, play charades, and develop games. Create a skit using terms, names, and other details that you need to remember. Improvise by using zany associations within the skit and act it out to reinforce remembering.

Kinesthetic

○ To remember steps for a problem or process, such as with math and science course work, use index cards for each step. Arrange the cards in the correct order.

○ To strengthen recall of abstract concepts, imagine related lab experiments, computer programs, field trips, photographs, and the like.

Your Personal Action Statement

1. I will: _____

_____

_____

2. My greatest hurdle to achieving this is: _____

_____

_____

3. I will eliminate this hurdle by: _____

_____

_____

4. My time plan for achieving this is: _____

_____

_____

5. My reward for achieving this is: _____

_____

_____

Conclusion

The grid in Figure 6.4 lists the memory techniques presented in this chapter. As part of the end-of-chapter comprehension check, summarize the techniques by completing the chart: Add a description of the strategy, an example of how you've used it, and comments regarding its effectiveness. Add other strategies at the bottom.

Comprehension Check

1. Employ the technique of visualization by creating an illustration that answers the question, "How are sleep, time management, and memory connected?"
2. Describe a situation in which you used your senses to enhance your memory.

FIGURE **6.4**   *Summary grid.*

MEMORY STRATEGY	DESCRIPTION	EXAMPLE	COMMENTS
Adequate sleep			
Small blocks of time			
Review soon after			
Organize/ categorize			
Use your senses			
Association			
Mnemonic devices			
Other			

CHAPTER 7

Success with Tests

FOCUS QUESTIONS

How are test-taking anxiety, test preparation, and test-taking performance related?

Compare and contrast preparation for objective tests versus essay tests.

Describe three elements of test-wiseness that you will use this semester.

CHAPTER TERMS

After reading this chapter, define (in your own words) and provide an example for each of the following terms:

- deep muscle relaxation
- desensitization
- directive words
- mental imagery
- mental trigger
- performance anxiety
- qualifying words
- test anxiety
- test-wiseness

ESSENTIAL INGREDIENTS
College Studying

Success with Tests: Four Essential Ingredients

Although test performance cannot be guaranteed, there are definite steps you can take to improve your test-taking skills. Success with tests is based on four essential ingredients:

1. Be prepared.
2. Reduce your test anxiety.
3. Develop test-wiseness.
4. Review the test.

Be Prepared

KEEP UP WITH ACADEMIC WORK

Test preparation starts from the first day of the semester. Maintaining regular study *throughout each week* is a crucial element of test preparation, including study for online courses. The more complex the information, the more time you will need to process and understand course content adequately for an exam. If you have followed strategies suggested in previous chapters, you likely are ready to study (as opposed to cram) for the upcoming exam:

- Have you attended all classes and taken appropriate notes?
- Have you sought information about class sessions or assignments that you missed or were unsure about?
- Have you reviewed your notes soon after each class—clarifying, organizing, emphasizing, and summarizing key ideas?
- Have you kept pace with reading assignments, creating some type of study guide that represents important ideas?
- Have you reviewed weekly, either with a classmate, tutor, or study group, online discussion or by yourself?

If you answered yes to all or most of these questions, you have been integrating study with day-to-day academic demands and thus are well prepared for the next step: *reviewing* and *consolidating* subject matter before the exam.

DEVELOP TEST REVIEW GUIDES

Plan for added study time each day during the week before a major test. During this added time, select, combine, and organize key information from class notes and readings and create concise review guides. Look for the major topics, often repeated in both readings and class notes; then dissect these major topics into related subtopics. Think about how the topics are connected. For example,

- Topic A is *part of* topic B.
- Topic A is *the opposite of* topic B.
- Topic A *results in* topic B.
- Topic B is *an example of* topic A.
- Topic B *describes* topic A.
- Topic B is *a function of* topic A.

Because test items often reflect these topics and connections, make sure they are part of your study guide, as illustrated in the following pages.

Study cards (Figure 7.1) are useful when you expect to have many terms or concepts on an upcoming test. On an index card, write the term or concept on the front and a summary, definition, explanation, or other associated ideas on the back. Study cards are effective for test review because they are handy and flexible; use them to review while waiting in line, between classes or appointments, in a bus or car, and so on.

Study cards to review for psychology test.   FIGURE **7.1**

OBSERVATION

Study behavior in natural setting.

Adv: normal setting

Disadv: no cause/effect

CASE STUDIES

Info. gathered about specific individuals.

Adv: detailed

Disadv: a lot of time

FIGURE **7.2**   *Review chart for history test.*

"VIETNAM: Progression of Events"

Vietnam Events	WHAT is it?/WHY important?	WHO?	WHEN?
Domino Theory (escalation)	Like row of dominoes—if one country falls, so will the rest.	Eisenhower	1954
Dien Bien Phu (escalation)	French troops parachute into a fort; terrible loss; only 200 of 1,400 escape.	French	1954
"Flexible Response" (escalation)	2,000 "advisors" going to Vietnam to research what is going on.	JFK	1960
Gulf of Tonkin (escalation)	Advises the president to take "all necessary measures."	LBJ	Aug. 1964
Tet Offensive (escalation)	Widens the scope of the war.		1968
"Peace with Honor" (withdrawal)	Nixon's election slogan—take U.S. troops out of Vietnam w/ honor.	Nixon	Nov. 1968
My Lai Massacre (withdrawal)	Public outrage w/ revelations that U.S. soldiers massacre 500 noncombative civilians.	U.S. soldiers; Charlie Team; William Calley	March 1968 breaks in Dec.
The Pentagon Papers (withdrawal)	Reveals everything about the war.	Daniel Ellsberg	June 1971

[Contributed by Melissa Swope]

Maps and charts (Figure 7.2) are effective tools for test review because they help you select, organize, and categorize important ideas and details in a visual format—key strategies for enhancing your recall of information.

REHEARSE FOR THE EXAM

Practice Test Questions. Prepare for an upcoming exam by answering questions similar to the type of questions that you expect to be on the test. By completing practice questions, you are reviewing the subject matter while familiarizing your-self with the format of the test (i.e., essay, multiple choice, true/false, matching, identification, and/or sentence completion questions). Use the end-of-chapter or separate study guide questions, or create your own practice questions. If you participate in a study group, ask each person to make up practice questions to share with the others. For computerized tests, practice using a similar online format. In addition, practice with time constraints to build your speed and confidence for real timed exams.

"I am an English major; thus keeping up with the reading is of utmost importance. Most importantly, I try to attend all of my classes because a large part of the test questions seem to come straight from class sessions. The week before the test, I usually have the bulk of all material read, which leaves the last several days for review, reinforcement, and mini-quizzes. Lately, I have been feeling more confident about my learning, and my test scores reflect this." —KESHIA

Teach others. An additional type of rehearsal is to run through the material by teaching the information to another person. When you are able to explain information clearly to others, you likely know it. Convince a roommate, family member, or friend to be the designated student, or teach the material to yourself. In the role of teacher you will be training yourself to know the information thoroughly. At the very least, saying the information out loud will help reinforce what you do and do not know.

"First, I allow myself four to five days to study for a test. Second, I anticipate what questions may be on a test and then find a family member to 'teach' the subject matter to. By using these three strategies I have already increased my grade in two classes." —SAM

try it out!

1. Identify a *subject* in which you will be having a major exam in the near future.
2. In *preparation* for the exam, answer the following questions:
   • When is the exam?
   • What topics and material are to be covered in the exam?

- What type of questions will be on the exam?
- Have you been keeping up with course work for this subject? If not, where have you been falling behind and what do you still need to do?

3. Continue preparing for the exam by creating a *test review guide*, either study cards or a map or chart.
4. Next, develop a *practice exam*, using questions similar to the type you expect to be on the real exam.
5. Continue *rehearsing* for the exam by teaching key concepts to another person.
6. After you have taken the exam, **Assess Your Success** with the methods of preparation you used for this test.

Critical
Thinking
Task

- Which preparation strategies did you find to be especially effective and why?
- Which strategies were *not* effective for you? Why?
- How will you approach preparation for the next exam in this subject?

Reduce Test Anxiety

DO YOU HAVE TEST ANXIETY?

Preparation is a key factor in reducing extreme worry and anxiousness associated with taking a test. However, at times, even the best prepared student gets trapped in a cycle of excessive anxiety. **Test anxiety,** a type of **performance anxiety,** is based on the apprehensive thoughts and emotional feelings associated with how well you will do on an exam.

Consider this example: Two people look outside and see bright sunlight. One person thinks, "Great weather! I can't wait to go swimming today!" He feels lively and full of energy. Another person sees the same bright sunlight but thinks, "Darn it—I have to water the grass and flowers again today." He feels lethargic and moves slowly. These two people have completely different thoughts—and subsequent physical feelings—about the same situation.

Similarly, people have differences in thoughts and physical reactions in regard to test taking. One student might think of an exam as a personal challenge, whereas another thinks of the same exam as a personal threat. It is the latter student who worries, often excessively, about the test and, as a consequence, often exhibits physical symptoms of anxiety.

your THOUGHTS [worry]

↓ lead to ↓

your PHYSICAL REACTION [anxiety]

Test-taking anxiety is a condition that interferes with positive test results. How anxious are you when taking a test? Would you have performed better if you weren't so uneasy and fearful? The nearby "Try It Out!" will provide an estimate of your level of test anxiety.

try it out!

Test Anxiety Assessment

Complete by checking *Yes*, *Sometimes*, or *No* for each of the twelve statements:

WHEN PREPARING FOR OR TAKING A TEST:	YES	SOMETIMES	NO
1. I think about whether I'm going to pass or fail.	○	○	○
2. I keep wishing the exam was over.	○	○	○
3. I worry that I am not doing well.	○	○	○
4. I can't stop thinking about how nervous I feel.	○	○	○
5. My stomach gets upset.	○	○	○
6. My heart beats very fast.	○	○	○
7. I often freeze up, and my mind goes blank.	○	○	○
8. I feel hot and sweaty.	○	○	○
9. I feel very tense.	○	○	○
10. I forget information that I really know.	○	○	○
11. I often get panicky.	○	○	○
12. I tend to breathe faster.	○	○	○

SCORING – Total your points using the following key:

Each *Yes* = 2 points
Each *Sometimes* = 1 point
Each *No* = 0 points
Your total points = _____

(You'll have a total score between 0 and 24.)

The higher your total score on the Test Anxiety Assessment, the more anxious you are when taking a test. If your score is between 10 and 24, you'll likely benefit from working on strategies to reduce the worry and anxiety associated with test taking.

Note that items 1 through 4 on the questionnaire refer to those thoughts that impact negatively on your test-taking performance. Worry over your test results, whether you are going to pass the course, whether you will make it through college, or even your parents' reactions can interfere with test performance. Excessive worry can lead to a physical reaction toward test taking, including sweaty palms, rapid breathing, dizziness, and so on. Assessment items 5 through 12 refer to this physical response. Thus apprehension plus a physiological response results in full-blown test anxiety.

Keep in mind that not all worry and anxiety is bad. In fact, *some* anxiousness can be good in that it keeps your adrenaline flowing and, as a result, gives you that edge to perform better. However, you do not want your anxiety to be excessive to the point where it interferes with your performance. If you think that you could have done better on a test if you weren't so anxious, you need to tackle ways to reduce this anxiety.

Critical Thinking Task

pause... *and reflect*

Refer back to your total score on the Test Anxiety Assessment.

- If your total score is less than 10: Reflect about why your anxiety is low. Consider how you approach a test—that is, how you *think* about exams and what you *do* that keeps anxiety at a minimum. Why don't you worry excessively?
- If your total score is 10 or above: Think about those *situations* that trigger worry and anxiety for you. Here are some circumstances that might set off anxiousness:
  - The word *test* on the syllabus or board.
  - The night before the exam.
  - The morning of the exam.
  - Walking into the classroom to take the exam.
  - Hearing other students talk about the exam.
  - The instructor passing out the exam to the class.
  - A test item that you're not sure how to answer.
  - Waiting to get back the results.

Come up with at least three or four scenarios that apply to you. Beside each scenario, write the *exact thoughts* that run through your mind when you are in that situation. For example, for the situation "A test item that you're not sure how to answer," you might have these thoughts: "Oh no, I'm going to fail!" or "I should know this answer," or "This is terrible!"

CHANGE HOW YOU THINK ABOUT THE TEST

One way to diminish feelings of test anxiety is to change your thoughts about tests.

Focus on the *present*, not the past or the future. Test-anxious students tend to focus their thoughts on what occurred previously ("I did poorly on the last quiz") or what they predict to occur ("I'm going to fail this test"). Bear in mind that your past performance does *not* foretell your present performance. Likewise, you cannot predict accurately what the outcome of a test will be. Therefore, keep your thoughts focused on the here and now, that is, your present place in time. Be alert to the thoughts that run through your head; if you begin to think about past or future events, *stop* and redirect your thoughts to what you are doing or can do *now*. Deter yourself from thinking about an imaginary future and, instead, think about the realistic present moment in time. For example,

"I did poorly on the last chemistry quiz and am going to fail this upcoming quiz."

↓ changes to ↓

"I am doing practice problems in anticipation of the next chemistry quiz."

Put the test in perspective. Test-anxious students tend to overinflate the importance of any single test. In the realm of worldly events, any one exam is not *that* important! Keep a realistic, less extreme perspective about quizzes and tests. Students sometimes are helped by playing out, in their minds, a frightening chain of events linked to test performance. This tactic produces scenarios that often are exaggerated and ridiculous. As an example, the following is the chain of thoughts for one anxious student:

"I am going to fail this biology test."

↓ which leads to ↓

"I am going to flunk the biology course."

↓ which leads to ↓

"I am going to be on academic probation."

↓ which leads to ↓

"I am going to flunk out of college."

↓ which leads to ↓

"I am going to be flipping hamburgers for the rest of my life!"

Ideally this student realizes that it is neither logical nor realistic to think that failing a biology test will result in a lifetime of flipping hamburgers. Being aware of unreasonable thinking patterns can help you maintain a more balanced view of a test.

Recognize your choices. "I *have to* do well" or "I *must* get an A" are common thoughts of students fretting over a test. These thoughts imply that the student has no other options *but* to perform well—or even perfectly! Practice eliminating the phrases "have to," "required to," "should," and "must" from your thoughts. Instead, replace them with phrases that suggest you have options, such as "I *prefer to* do well" or "I'd *rather* improve my score on the next exam." Mindfully choose words that evoke personal choices and the leeway and sense of freedom that comes with these choices.

Be positive. Be alert to your negative, and even apathetic, thoughts. Instead, focus on positive, encouraging aspects of yourself and your actions. Choose words that reflect optimism and personal affirmation. Also, seek encouragement from family and friends. As a result, you will feel more upbeat and confident about taking tests. For example,

"I'm so angry at myself for getting a C on this quiz!"

↓ is replaced with ↓

"It's *okay* that I received a C; I'll probably *improve* on the next quiz."

"I don't care what I do on this test!"

↓ is replaced with ↓

"I will try to earn a *reasonable grade* on this test."

Critical Thinking Task

pause... *and reflect*

Do you see yourself reflected in any of these thought patterns? Refer back to page 118 where you identified specific thoughts associated with testing situations. Using the previous suggestions for changing how you think about a test, create *new* statements to reflect a change in your own thought pattern.

CHANGE HOW YOU REACT PHYSICALLY TO A TEST

Because test-anxious students view the exam as threatening, their bodies react as in any other intimidating or frightening situation: Breathing becomes more shallow and rapid, the heart beats faster, muscles tense, adrenaline flows throughout the body, skin becomes sweaty, and digestion slows down. This physical reaction is appropriate when a situation is actually threatening, such as spotting an animal running in front of your car when you are driving. In that

"Since I'm usually well prepared for exams, you'd think that I'd be more relaxed come exam time. I just can't seem to walk into a room, knowing I'm going to take a test, and be calm. Deep breathing does help—some. I take a couple of breaths before I walk into the test room (at least I know I'm still breathing, right?). I think I'm hopeless, so the thing I do is talk to myself, which I've become a pro at. I just try to put each test into perspective. I point out that I am prepared, I've studied, and that one test won't blow my grade. This helps to bring me from 'high-strung' to just plain 'nervous,' but this isn't all bad. I think it's the perfectionist's advantage, being able to handle a nervous, pressure situation." —RACHEL

situation it *is* appropriate that your body becomes tense as you focus only on not hitting the animal. However, these same intense physical symptoms work *against* you when taking a test; tense muscles, rapid breathing, upset stomach, and so forth, can cause you to lose your concentration and mental acuity. Instead of focusing on the content of the exam, you become focused on your extreme and even frightening physical reactions. However, by using two simple techniques, **mental imagery** and **deep muscle relaxation,** you can greatly alter your physical response to a test.

Mental imagery. Your mind plays a powerful role in determining your physical response to an event. A calm, peaceful image in your mind can result in a tranquil, stress-free physical response. Think of an event in your own past that evokes a feeling of personal contentment, joy, or satisfaction. Use all of your senses to reconstruct a realistic version of this event. Imagine yourself in that situation: What are you specifically doing? What sounds do you hear? What are you saying? Can you smell or taste anything? What are you feeling? Because this situation activates a feeling of calm and contentment within you, it is called your **mental trigger.** Use this mental trigger often. Become accustomed to generating this mental image to prompt a response of easy relaxation.

Deep breathing and muscle relaxation. You likely tense your muscles when a stressful, threatening situation arises. This tense, rigid, bodily response can rapidly lead to feelings of panic, which result in poor test performance. With directed practice, you can train yourself how to replace the tense response with a calming response.

One type of deep muscle relaxation exercise begins with monitoring your breathing so you are mindful of slow, full, even breaths that originate deep in your abdomen (as opposed to shallow breaths originating in your upper chest). Do this exercise when you have a chunk of time by yourself, in a darkened, quiet room, with your eyes closed. Next, focus on relaxing your muscles from the top of your head down through the trunk of your body, your limbs, to your toes. Concentrate on one group of muscles at a time, letting these muscles become loose and relaxed. Picture your muscles becoming heavy, like a wet mop. By loosening your muscles, you will be calming your body. With practice over time, you will be able to create this feeling of deep relaxation easily and quickly and, as a result, free your mind to concentrate on tasks such as preparing for or taking an exam.

DESENSITIZE YOURSELF

Desensitization refers to a gradual, yet steady exposure to the anxiety-producing event. Desensitization begins by breaking down the event—in this case, test taking—into small and specific anxiety-producing situations. You place the situations in order: from *least* to *most* anxiety producing. Starting with the situation creating the least anxiety, you combine mental imagery (imagining yourself in the particular situation) with deep muscle relaxation techniques. Monitor your physical responses while you practice mentally being in the specific situation. Build toward real exposure of the test-taking situation; continue to monitor both your mental and physical reactions.

As an example, one student identified the following scenarios as producing varying levels of personal anxiety:

> "I have some anxiousness when I hear the instructor announce the date of the test. I then worry every time I see the word *test* in my planner. My anxiety really increases a few days before the test when I begin to study more. I have trouble sleeping the night before a major test. The peak of my anxiety is when I enter the classroom the day of the test!"

This student's anxiety builds for each succeeding scenario. For desensitization, the student begins with the *least anxiety-producing scenario:* "the instructor announces the date of the test." While in a state of deep muscle relaxation, the student creates a mental image of being in a specific classroom and hearing the instructor announce a test date. The student rehearses thought patterns that counter anxiety, such as "I'll prepare for this test the best that I can." The student repeats this image and related thoughts until he notices that his response is continually calm. At this point, he continues with desensitization by imagining the *next higher scenario*: "seeing the word *test* in my planner." He continues until his calm, relaxed responses readily translate to real-life test scenarios.

"Taking a test used to be one of my worst nightmares; I had almost every symptom of test anxiety. I used to get so mad for allowing myself to get so upset. I created so much pressure for myself, including whether I would pass or fail, how low my GPA was, that the instructor hated me, how dumb I felt, I should have studied more, etc.—all of which affected the way I took a test. I was so relieved to find ways to overcome the fear of a test.

The first improvement I made was to complete my studying on a daily basis, instead of cramming during an all-night study binge. By covering the material regularly, I don't feel the need to cram and my anxiety has greatly diminished. I begin preparing for a test by reviewing my notes several days in advance. Now, when reviewing I am able to recall important ideas readily, which makes studying less of a problem. If I do begin to feel tense, I relax myself by taking deep breaths. To counter my fear of professors, I ask questions either after class or during office hours. This permits me to feel more comfortable with taking a test." **—SHANA**

Problem
Solving
Task

pause... *and reflect*

1. Refer to Figure 7.3. In the left-hand column, place a check mark in the circle beside each of the listed situations that result in some level of worry or anxiety for you.
2. Order the circles with check marks, from least anxiety producing (write a 1 on the line next to that circle) to most anxiety producing.
3. To the right of each item with a check mark, write at least one way you can reduce anxiety by changing your thoughts, your actions, and/or your preparation techniques.

FIGURE **7.3**   *Reducing test anxiety.*

Causes of Test Worry and Anxiety	Ways to Reduce or Eliminate
○ _____ The first test of the semester.	
○ _____ The test counts toward a big chunk of the final grade.	
○ _____ The test covers lots of material.	
○ _____ I don't fully understand the material.	
○ _____ I don't feel prepared for the test.	
○ _____ I don't feel competent with the type of questions.	
○ _____ I allowed too little time for studying for the test.	
○ _____ I am taking more than one test during the day.	
○ _____ I've previously performed poorly in the course.	
○ _____ I'm afraid that I'm going to forget key information.	
○ _____ I feel pressure to get a good grade in the course.	
○ _____ I'm thinking about my parents' or instructor's expectations.	
○ _____ I'm concerned about my overall GPA.	
○ _____ I'm afraid of failing.	
○ _____ I'm concerned about my future job prospects.	
○ _____ Any other?	

try it out!

1. Use *mental imagery*: In your mind, identify and recreate a scene that triggers a sense of calmness.
2. Combine your mental image with *deep muscle relaxation*. Practice breathing and relaxing all of your muscles systematically. Do this exercise at least twice a day for 15- to 30-minute sessions when you are able to turn off lights, be comfortable, and not be disturbed by others.
3. Practice *desensitization*. Begin with the least anxiety-producing situation that you previously identified.
4. **Assess Your Success** by answering the following questions:
   - How have you progressed with the process just described? Explain your progress with each step.
   - After completing a test or quiz, have you noticed a reduction in your worry and anxiety? Describe the test-taking situation and your reaction.
   - What will you continue to do to decrease your anxiety?

Develop Test-Wiseness

Test-wiseness refers to the skills and strategies related to *how to take* tests. It involves becoming familiar with and savvy about answering various types of questions: objective (true/false, multiple choice, matching, sentence completion) and essay. When used in combination with (not as a substitute for) thorough, sound preparation, test-wiseness can noticeably improve your test-taking performance.

USE A FIVE-STEP COURSE OF ACTION

Step 1. Have supplies ready, including pen/pencils, extra paper (if allowed), and a watch to use for monitoring time. Assume that you will have to turn off your cell phone and other telecommunication devices while taking the exam.

Step 2. Before looking at the test itself, use the back of the paper, the margins, or blank scratch paper to jot down details that are crammed into your head and you are afraid of forgetting. This step will (1) unburden your mind of those nagging details, and (2) provide you with a means to focus your attention immediately and involve yourself in the test-taking process.

Step 3. Prior to answering any questions, quickly look over the entire test and note the

- Length of the test.
- Types of questions and point value attached to each type.
- General difficulty level.

Also, carefully read the test instructions. Based on this information, strategize about how to approach the test given your time constraints. Generally, start with questions you can answer more readily or are worth more points; then tackle the difficult, time-consuming items.

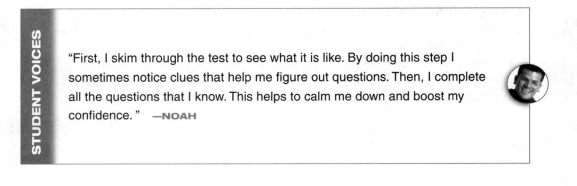

STUDENT VOICES

"First, I skim through the test to see what it is like. By doing this step I sometimes notice clues that help me figure out questions. Then, I complete all the questions that I know. This helps to calm me down and boost my confidence. " **—NOAH**

pause.... *and reflect*

"Begin with objective questions, and then answer any essay questions."
    Why is this strategy generally recommended for test taking? Do you agree with this suggestion? Why or why not?

Step 4. After completing questions you are sure of, go back and answer those questions that you left blank or put a question mark beside. At this point, you will be calmer and your mind will be clearer, allowing you to concentrate on how to answer the more difficult questions. Furthermore, now you might see clues to help you answer the questions you initially left blank.

Step 5. When you complete all items, go back and check for mistakes. Reread the test directions; you might discover that, in your haste, you misread directions the first time. Then, slowly reread each question. Use your *mouth*, though not your voice, to read and silently hear each question and answer. This technique will help you to check vigilantly for oversights and errors.

Note that for some online tests, you will be unable to do steps 3 through 5. Various online exams are set up so you *must* answer the questions in the order they appear on the screen. You cannot skip items and you cannot go back through the test. Therefore, before beginning an online test, confirm the setup; see if you can answer questions in the order of your choosing and if you can go back through the test before finishing.

WATCH FOR KEY WORDS

Pay attention to word choices in test questions. Look for key words or phrases in both objective and essay questions that pinpoint requirements for a correct answer. As an example, examine the following multiple-choice test question:

> **"What is the main effect of the Hitler Jugend on events leading to the Holocaust?"**

"Main effect" is the first key phrase; it implies that, although there may be many effects, your instructor is looking for the main, or foremost, effect. In addition, the word *effect* indicates you are searching for a cause-and-effect connection between ideas. In other words, when answering this question, consider how "_____ results in _____."

Other key words are the *terms* associated with the subject or topic. For this question, *Hitler Jugend* and *Holocaust* are the crucial terms that complete the cause- and-effect connection and thus are central to the correct answer.

Critical Thinking Task

pause.... *and reflect*

For the following test questions, identify the key words. Note *why* each key word is important for providing the correct answer.

1. "What was the Final Solution, and who proposed it?"
2. "Number the events in the order in which they occurred."
3. "List three similarities and three differences between World War I and World War II."
4. "What statement best describes the long-term effects of the post–World War II tension between the United States and Russia?"
5. "Choose three statements that accurately describe how married life and family income was affected by the influx of women into the workforce after World War II."

LOOK FOR QUALIFYING WORDS

Qualifying words are words or phrases that moderate an extreme idea in a statement. They indicate that the statement's message is *not* a hard-and-fast rule. The presence of qualifying words suggests that exceptions, omissions, misstatements, or errors are possible. Consider a continuum (Figure 7.4) with "absolute" and "extreme" words at either end: absolutely "yes" at one end and absolutely "no" at the other. In between the ends are the vast majority of qualifying words indicating moderation, possible oversights, special conditions, and so on.

Some messages *do* belong to one extreme or the other: "The earth *always* rotates on its axis" or "A human being *certainly* is not a reptile." Both of these statements contain extreme words and both happen to be true statements. However, most events fall somewhere in between the extreme ends:

- "It *definitely* rains in June." = FALSE
- "It *never* rains in June." = FALSE
- "It *usually* rains in June." = TRUE (This statement allows for the one June 50 years ago in which we had absolutely no rain.)

Many (not all) statements containing qualifying words happen to be true statements. Therefore, if you are not sure of the correct answer when reading a true/false statement on a test, use these tips:

- If qualifying words are present, the statement tends to be true.
- If absolute, extreme words are present, the statement often is false.

Remember: This method does *not* replace studying and knowing subject matter. Consider this as a guide to assist you when you are stuck, not as a hard-and-fast rule.

FIGURE **7.4** *Qualifying words.*

definitely absolutely	usually	somewhat	maybe	sometimes	perhaps	in my judgment	never have to
YES		IN-BETWEEN 'QUALIFYING WORDS'					**NO**
always certainly	most	typically	possibly	generally	to some extent	in my opinion	none

try it out!

Mark the following statements as either true or false. *Why* did you answer each item as you did? What *qualifying words* can you identify?

___ 1. In the year 2150, the projected worldwide life expectancy will be 86 years old.

___ 2. The world's crude-oil reserves likely will run out by the year 2063.

___ 3. The belief that smoking threatens a person's health is not linked to that person's beliefs about the severity of cancer.

___ 4. You should plan for some leisure activity during the day—everybody needs a break.

___ 5. Stress plays a role in all physical illness because of its effect on the immune system.

PRACTICE MULTIPLE-CHOICE QUESTIONS

Multiple-choice questions are the most popular type of test question, particularly in large introductory-level courses. Think of multiple-choice questions as a series of true/false statements: The lead-in clause or statement is combined with each option, forming a series of longer statements that are either true or false. Your task, as the test taker, is to choose the *best* true option. Here's a sample question:

1. In a test question, "compare" refers to
   A. A list of items.
   B. A relationship among items.
   C. Similarities among items.
   D. A + B.
   E. None of the above.
   F. All of the above.

By combining the lead-in clause with each of the six options, there are essentially six "true/false" statements for this one question:

   A. In a test question, "compare" refers to a list of items.
   B. In a test question, "compare" refers to a relationship among items.
   C. In a test question, "compare" refers to similarities among items.
   D. In a test question, "compare" refers to a list of items and a relationship among items.
   E. . . . and so on.

Note that options A through C are central to the answer because the remaining three options (D through F) are various combinations of the first three choices. Thus you should focus on the first three statements (A through C) and identify each as being true *or* false:

A. In a test question, "compare" refers to a list of items.
[*This statement is false.*]

B. In a test question, "compare" refers to a relationship among items.
[*This statement is true because a relationship or connection does exist in a comparison.*]

C. In a test question, "compare" refers to similarities among items.
[*This statement is definitely true because "compare" means "like" or "similar to."*]

You are searching for the *one* true statement as the answer. Given that you identified two true statements, look at the remaining three choices to see if "B + C" is an option. Only "A + B" is presented, and you can eliminate this option (D) because it is a false statement. Likewise, both options E and F have to be false (because at *least one* but *not all* of statements A through C are true). Thus choose option C as your *best answer*.

In summary, viewing multiple-choice items as a series of true/false statements can simplify your test-taking approach, especially when multiple combinations are present as options. As you read the lead-in clause with each option, write "T" or "F" beside that option, with the goal of ultimately choosing the one "T." If you have more than one "T," then look at the combinations, ultimately choosing the *best* option as your answer.

Strategies for choosing which option is best and which options can be eliminated are summarized next. If you are not sure of the so-called best answer on a test, these strategies will help you to make *informed guesses*:

1. Select the more *specific and inclusive* choice (this often is the longest option). Eliminate extremely general options.

2. Eliminate *grammatical mismatches* when combining the lead-in clause with an option, such as a plural subject with a singular verb.

   Example for strategies 1 and 2: When setting career goals for yourself

   A. Evaluate your options, including personal, emotional, and monetary costs. [*includes more specific information*]

   B. Career goals can be determined later. [*too general; not grammatically correct when read with the lead-in clause*]

   Option A is the best answer.

3. Select an option that is *similar in format* to others, such as containing repeated terms, a similar structure, or the same word pattern.

   Example for strategy 3: Research demonstrates that people who practice deep muscle relaxation

   A. Exhibit decreases in psychological well-being.

   B. Show little difference from the control group.

C. Exhibit increases in psychological well-being. [*options A and C are similar in format*]

   Option C is the best answer.

4. If a *word or phrase is repeated* throughout the test, it tends to be part of a true option at some point.

5. Focus on *familiar terminology* as possible true options. Instructors sometimes use vocabulary that does not relate to the subject matter; if you have never seen the term before, consider it a false option.

   Example for strategies 4 and 5: Deep breathing consists of

   A. Adrenaline flowing through your body.
   B. Full, even breaths originating in your abdomen. [*repetition of "breathing" and "breaths"*]

   Option B is the best answer.

6. When "*not*" is part of the lead-in clause, eliminate "not" when reading the statement and then search for the false option.

   Example for strategy 6: Which is not a benefit of meditation? *is changed to* Which is a benefit of meditation?

   A. Improved mood. [*true*]
   B. Increased heart rate. [*false*]
   C. Increased energy. [*true*]

   Option B is the best answer.

7. Be aware of *qualifying words*, often indicating true statements, and *absolute words*, often indicating false statements (see Figure 7.4).

   Example for strategy 7: Deep breathing

   A. Tends to elevate moods. [*"tends to" is a qualifying phrase*]
   B. Definitely decreases depression and anxiety. [*"definitely" is an absolute word*]

   Option A is the best answer.

8. A *middle option* tends to be correct more times than do beginning or ending options, especially when presented with a range of numbers.

   Example for strategy 8: College students should have how many hours of sleep per night?

   A. 6–8 hours
   B. 8–10 hours
   C. 9–11 hours

   Option B is the best answer.

9. "All the above" is more often true; "none of the above" is more often false. Instructors prefer testing students about what is *present* on paper ("all of the above"), as opposed to what is *missing* ("none of the above").

10. If you are not sure, use your background knowledge, experiences, and common sense!

> Example for strategies 9 and 10: You can reduce levels of stress by
> A. Physical exercise. [*true*]
> B. The support of friends or family. [*true*]
> C. A forgiving and hopeful frame of mind. [*not sure, but I'll consider it "true" because it makes sense*]
> D. All the above.
> E. None of the above.
>   Option D is the best answer.

11. If you are *not* being penalized for wrong answers, then don't leave an answer blank. You might as well *guess!*

try it out!

Critical Thinking Task

What is the *best* answer for each of the following multiple-choice questions? Write your reasons for selecting or eliminating options, using the previous list of strategies.

1. "Soy isolate" is
   A. A white powdered food that is 90% protein.
   B. A white powdered food that is 90% carbohydrate.
   C. A chemical compound used in kitchen utensils.
   D. A + B

2. The characteristics of "microtubules" include:
   A. They have a shape of straight, hollow tubes.
   B. They have a shape of solid rods.
   C. They have a size of approximately 25 nm.
   D. A + B
   E. A + C
   F. All of the above.

3. Which operations are associated with the information-processing model of memory?
   A. Input, storage, and retrieval
   B. Input, rehearsal, and output
   C. Process, storage, and recall
   D. Encode, consolidate, and retrieval

4. In one research study, college students had more accurate memories:
   A. The students needed repetitive coaxing.
   B. The students did not have more accurate memories.

   C. When they exhibited abnormal disorders.
   D. When they had high blood sugar levels.

5. An instructional method that does *not* enhance creative thought is
   A. Establishing preset rules.
   B. Establishing collaborative learning groups.
   C. Using illustrations.

PRACTICE ESSAY QUESTIONS

Expect to encounter essay questions, especially in social science courses and in smaller higher-level courses. Instructors often expect students to exhibit higher-level thought processes when answering essay questions.

Critical Thinking Task

Have a clear understanding of **directive words,** those specific words in essay questions signaling *what the instructor expects in your answer*. Directive words orient you as to what to include and *how to organize* your answer. Test your knowledge of directive words by completing the second column in Figure 7.5. (The first item is done for you.)

The following steps provide a general guideline to assist you with successfully completing essay-type test items.

Step 1. Be clear on the *type* and *length* of answer that your instructor expects.

- For a short answer essay question, expect to write one to two paragraphs for your answer.
- For a longer essay question, write several substantial paragraphs, amounting to one or more pages in length.

Step 2. Read the question and *jot down your immediate thoughts*. What terms and ideas do you associate with the question?

Step 3. Circle or underline *key words* within the question, including *directive words*, such as those in Figure 7.5, and words or terms *linked* to the topic.

Step 4. Reflect on the *ideas* that will adequately answer the question, writing a draft as you move along:

- Decide about the main idea of your answer; then draft a *thesis statement* representing this main idea. Use key words in the question to form your introductory statement.
- Decide about appropriate *supporting ideas* and how to *organize* these ideas. What information will you include that explains, supports, or relates to your thesis?
- Decide about *specific evidence* or *examples* that make your answer more accurate and precise.

FIGURE **7.5** *Directive words.*

Directive Words	What I Should Include in My Answer
Compare	*similarities* between/among ideas; how "things" are **alike** (can also include differences)
Contrast	
Define	
Critique	
Describe	
Discuss	
Explain	
Evaluate	
Identify	
Illustrate	
Justify	
List	
Relate	
Summarize	
Trace	

- Refer back to your immediate jottings (step 2). Should you add any of these initial thoughts to your draft?

Step 5. Carefully read through your draft, mouthing the words so you will see and hear your ideas.

- Does your answer make sense? Are you answering completely?
- Are you accurate yet concise? (Do not pad your answer with excessive details—consider the impression your answer will make on your instructor, who will be reading a stack of similar answers!)
- Do your ideas flow smoothly—that is, are you connecting thoughts to increase the fluency of ideas?

Step 6. Read your answer backward so you concentrate on each word and catch any spelling errors.

Figure 7.6 shows a question, a breakdown of the six-step process, and a sample answer.

Sample essay question and answer.   FIGURE **7.6**

"Compare and contrast the leadership of Franklin D. Roosevelt and Adolf Hitler."

Step 1:   The instructor expects some detail and/or examples to explain the main idea; length is approximately two to three paragraphs, 250–300 words.

Step 2:   Immediate thoughts that the student associated with the question:

FDR—U. S. president; well liked, especially by lower class; New Deal to reverse Depression and poverty; optimistic; bad economic times.

Hitler—Germany; dictator; pessimistic; used Jews and others as scape-goats; bad economic times; well liked.

Step 3:   Identify key words in the question.

"Compare and *contrast* the leadership of Franklin D. *Roosevelt* and Adolf *Hitler."*

Step 4:   (A) Create a thesis statement:

Roosevelt and Hitler were important world leaders but had different backgrounds and actions.

(B) Identify supporting ideas with specifics in chronological order:

- FDR born wealthy; Hitler born to civil servants.
- Both school dropouts.
- American and German people's resentment—Hoover administration (U. S.) and Weimar Republic (Germany).
- Initially, both not considered capable of leading.
- Democracy vs. dictatorship.
- Both had psychological influence on the public, emphasizing the current economic hardships and gaining popularity/support from the lower class.
- Roosevelt sympathized with the poor; he was honest about the present economic hardships but optimistic about the future—hope and confidence.
- Hitler emphasized hatred and violence against Jews, communists, the wealthy, and minorities, focusing on fears and projecting images of strength, power, and hard work.

(continued)

FIGURE **7.6**   *Continued.*

- Both used radio for propaganda: Roosevelt—weekly "Fireside Chat" for intimate connections with people. Hitler mandated radios; broadcast explosive speeches in front of cheering crowds.

(C) Identify connecting thoughts for "compare" and "contrast": similar; opposing; although; both; on the other hand; whereas; in contrast; different from; and; furthermore

After doing **Step 5** (carefully reading through the draft and revising) and **Step 6** (reading backward to catch spelling errors), the student completed the answer:

Completed Answer

Franklin Roosevelt and Adolf Hitler were significant world leaders who had both similar and opposing backgrounds, personality characteristics, and leadership styles. Roosevelt was born to a wealthy and influential political family of New York. On the other hand, Hitler was a child of a minor civil servant in Austria; he adopted Germany as his homeland later on. Both shared experiences as school dropouts and spent some perplexing years before they found their niche in politics.

Their rise to power in the 1933 elections was a result of resentment by the American and German people—resentment against the Hoover administration in the United States and against the Weimar Republic in Germany. Initially, both leaders were not considered to be capable of their new positions. Under Hitler, a one-party dictatorship was established, whereas Roosevelt led a democratic government in the United States.

Both Hitler and Roosevelt had great psychological influence on the public. Both emphasized the current economic hardships, gaining popularity and support from the lower class of their countries. Roosevelt sympathized with the poor; he was honest about the present economic hardships but optimistic about the future. He infused the American people with hope and confidence. In contrast, Hitler's popularity was built on a platform of hatred and violence against Jews, communists, the wealthy, and other minorities. He focused on people's fears, projecting images of strength, power, and hard work to counter those fears.

Furthermore, both leaders masterfully used the radio for broadcasting propaganda. Roosevelt hosted a weekly "Fireside Chat" to make intimate connections with the American people. Hitler mandated that all households in Germany have radios. Different from Roosevelt in style, only Hitler's explosive speeches in front of cheering crowds were broadcast to the German people.

In summary, Franklin Roosevelt and Adolf Hitler were influential world leaders who, though outwardly different, shared a number of leadership traits.

[Contributed by Yue Ying Zhang]

try it out!

Critical Thinking Task

For practice and as part of the chapter comprehension check, write a short essay answer for each focus question at the beginning of this chapter. Then critique your answer using the following criteria:

- Do you have a clearly written thesis statement that begins your answer? Establish your main idea at the start of your essay. This will focus your thoughts as the writer and your instructor's thoughts as the reader. When grading the tests, your instructor will be looking for key ideas in each of many essay exams. Therefore, make sure your key ideas are clearly stated at the start of your essay.
- Have you provided supporting ideas for your thesis statement? Include adequate and accurate details (examples, evidence, characteristics, explanations) to strengthen your ideas.
- Are your ideas organized?
- Have you made appropriate transitions between ideas? Include words such as *also, in addition, for example, such as, on the other hand, first, second, then, next, therefore, as a result, in summary.*
- Have you included a simple, tightly worded conclusion? End with a simple rewording of the thesis.
- Is your answer clearly written without padding extra words or ideas?
- Is the essay easy to read and understand?
- Is your essay free of all spelling and grammar errors?

Remember: Your instructor will be reading many answers to the same question. Therefore, strive to create an answer that correctly and distinctively illustrates your understanding of the subject matter.

Review the Test

The often-heard adage is true: You *do* learn from your mistakes! Receiving a test score is not enough; go back over test items, especially those that you answered incorrectly, in an effort to improve your performance on the next test for that course. If your instructor does not pass back the exam or does not use class time to review common errors, make an appointment to review your test during the instructor's office hours. Sometimes instructors allow students to go over test material with a graduate teaching assistant, trusted tutor, or a faculty member specializing in learning skills.

When reviewing your test, study how the test items are constructed. Most test items require more than pure memorization. Instead, you are required to relate ideas, apply concepts, distinguish similarities or differences, identify effects, or examine case studies. Taking the time and effort to review a previous test carefully is a valuable strategy in preparing you for the next test. As you continue to take class notes, read, and do assignments for a course, think ahead to the next exam: What will you need to know and how will the information be presented on the test?

In addition, when reviewing a test pay special attention to your errors. Generally, mistakes are related to one or more of the following causes:

- **Insufficient preparation:** not understanding and remembering the content well enough.
- **Inadequate test-taking skills:** not knowing how to approach the particular types of questions on the test. Or, in the case of online tests, being unfamiliar with the technology or uncomfortable with the setup of the exam.
- **Extreme anxiety:** a reaction that interferes with your test performance.

As you examine what you did right and wrong on the test, consider (1) what you can do to prepare yourself better for the next test, and (2) where you can go or who you can see for added support and guidance (your instructor, a study group, learning center, tutorial center, computer lab, or counseling center).

Critical Thinking Task

pause... *and reflect*

Identify a recent test that you will review, either in or out of class. Spend time carefully examining your responses. Do you recognize patterns of how you tend to approach and answer questions? *Why* did you make errors on this test (insufficient preparation, inadequate test-taking skills, or extreme anxiety)? *How* will you prepare for your next test?

try it out!

Learning Style and Test Taking

The following steps will help you decide how you best prepare for and take an exam:

1. Using Figure 7.7, in the right column circle your dominant learning preference—*visual, aural, read/write, or kinesthetic.* If you are multidimensional, that is, dominant in more than one modality, circle all that apply.

Test-taking strategies and learning preferences.

FIGURE **7.7**

TEST-TAKING STRATEGIES   **LEARNING PREFERENCES**

○ So that you are better able to form a mental picture of information, choose a study location away from others and free of distractions.

○ Develop test review guides that organize and categorize information, such as an idea map, timeline, chart, or graph.

○ If the exam consists of essay questions, use models of sample answers for practice.

○ Create visual cues for information that you anticipate needing to know for an exam.   **Visual**

○ To remember steps for a problem or process, develop a flowchart or diagram that separates each step.

○ Get an *overview* of the test before starting: **(1)** read the directions thoroughly; **(2)** note the number, type, and point value of questions; and **(3)** develop a strategy for tackling the test within designated time constraints.

○ Create a catchy rhyme, jingle, or song as a memory technique.

○ Go to the instructor, review sessions, or peer tutoring. Ask questions and participate in discussion.

○ *Teach others* the material; this will reinforce what you know. Or, debate others as a method of reviewing information.

○ Review class and lecture information by creating essay and multiple-choice questions, which tend to be your strength.   **Aural**

○ To remember steps for a problem or process, talk out loud through each step.

○ After finishing a test, go back and review your answers, looking for careless errors. As you review, read the items to yourself, moving your mouth.

○ Develop a written plan for how to study. Write down a time, place, and method of studying.

○ Silently reread notes, text materials, and manuals.

○ Create test review guides by rewriting notes and making lists. Turn illustrations and graphic materials into lists and statements.   **Read/write**

○ To help remember details, use the first letter of words to develop a word or phrase.

○ Use multiple-choice practice tests.

(continued)

FIGURE **7.6**   *Continued.*

○ After finishing a test, go back and review your answers, looking for careless errors. Carefully go over answers by moving your mouth and saying each word and moving your fingers from word to word.

○ Use a study location with adequate space to spread out.

○ Pace and move about while studying. Have a worry stone or stress ball in your hand.

○ Schedule extra practice and study time in a laboratory setting. Seek out case studies, computer programs, lab experiments, and/or photographs as a means to understand complex terms and abstract concepts.

○ Use role playing as a means to review for exams. Present the information to a classmate or family member. Create a "game show" that reviews information.

○ Create three-dimensional models as a means of review.   **Kinesthetic**

○ Use blackboards or whiteboards to develop practice tests items, make graphic representations of information, or play a game on the board with classmates.

○ Essay tests can be your weakness; practice these.

○ Learn how to tackle long, complicated multiple-choice items, including how to eliminate options and take educated guesses. Practice using ready-made study guides and end-of-chapter questions.

○ Carefully review the test after completing all questions. As you review, move your finger from word to word across the page as you go back over each item.

2. Refer to the strategies beside each of your preferences and place a check in the circles next to those that you do use regularly.

Critical
Thinking
Task

3. Identify a specific test-taking strategy that you will try for an upcoming exam. Write a Personal Action Statement for the strategy.

4. After taking the test **Assess Your Success**:
   • Did you follow through and reward yourself accordingly? Explain.
   • Did the hurdle materialize and did you manage it effectively? Explain.
   • What other changes do you want to make before your next quiz or exam?

Your Personal Action Statement

Identify an upcoming test: _____

1. I will: _____

   _____

   _____

2. My greatest hurdle to achieving this is: _____

   _____

   _____

3. I will eliminate this hurdle by: _____

   _____

   _____

4. My time frame for achieving this is: _____

   _____

   _____

5. My reward for achieving this is: _____

   _____

Conclusion

A myriad of factors intertwine to produce successful test results. As test time approaches for each subject, review the following questions as a reminder of strategies that will provide you with the advantages associated with successful test results.

ARE YOU SUFFICIENTLY PREPARED?

- Have you kept up with week-to-week class work, assignments, and regular review?
- Have you added extra study time the week before the exam?

- Have you reviewed and consolidated class notes and readings into a study guide?
- Have you practiced answering test questions?
- Have you taught and thoroughly discussed the subject matter with others?

IS YOUR TEST WORRY AND ANXIETY AT A MANAGEABLE LEVEL?

- Have you practiced strategies to reduce your anxiety in stressful test situations?
- Do you know how to calm both your thoughts and your physical reaction to a test?

ARE YOU KNOWLEDGEABLE ABOUT *HOW* TO TAKE TESTS?

- Do you know the steps to follow when taking the test?
- Have you practiced identifying key words in questions, including terms and qualifying words?
- Have you practiced how to answer multiple-choice questions, that is, how to eliminate incorrect options while choosing the best option?
- Have you practiced writing essays that answer the question correctly and clearly?

HAVE YOU REVIEWED YOUR CORRECTED TEST?

- Do you have a clear understanding of why answers are correct or incorrect?
- Did you discover why you made your errors?
- Have you considered ways to prepare yourself better for the next test?

Comprehension Check

evelop study cards for each chapter term on page 111. Write the term on the front of an index card and a brief explanation (in your own words) and example on the back.

CHAPTER 8

Continuing Your Academic Success
A REVIEW

FOCUS QUESTION

How can I continue to apply, monitor, and change my system of study?

CHAPTER TERM

After reading this chapter, define (in your own words) and provide an example for the following term:

- Personal Action Plan

ESSENTIAL INGREDIENTS College Studying

As outlined in Chapter 1, your success in college depends on a combination of factors: the learning strategies you choose to apply in and out of class, as well as your attitude and commitment to working hard and achieving your goals. The previous chapters provided a medley of strategies to build and strengthen your system of study. However, keep in mind that an effective system of study is not constant. Each term you will face a different set of academic assignments, personal demands, and social desires. At that point, do a personal appraisal of what strategies do and do not work for you. Adjust your study practices as needed to accommodate your varying courses, instructors, and requirements. The following suggestions will help you select and accomplish those adjustments and, as a result, continue on your path of academic success.

Your Personal Action Plan

For each major topic in the text, you chose a specific strategy to apply and then assess by means of a Personal Action Statement. The accumulation of your Personal Action Statements provides an overview of what you have put into practice this semester: What strategies you have used and how successful they have been for you. Now is the time to review your Personal Action Statements with the intent of combining and modifying them to create a global **Personal Action Plan,** an overview of learning behaviors and attitudes that are effective for you.

try it out!

Create a blueprint for your Personal Action Plan. Complete the three columns to create a personal profile of your study system.

Critical Thinking Task

1. **What I Do Well.** Note specific practices that have become a vital part of your learning and study methods.
2. **What I Will Change Now.** Jot down a definite strategy that likely will benefit you and you will put into practice. Remember: You are much more prone to follow through if you write down your intention.
3. **How Effective?** This column provides a quick means for follow-up. Note how effective or successful you were with each strategy that you tried.

My Personal Action Plan

	What I Do Well	What I Will Change Now	How Effective?
1. Managing my time • Use schedule, planner, and calendar. • Balance academic, personal, and social demands. • Reduce procrastination.			
2. Choosing a suitable study location • Minimize distractions. • Organize self, space, and materials.			
3. Selective and attentive listening in class • Create clear, correct, concise notes. • Review notes and create study guides.			
4. Understanding reading assignments • Preview before. • Break up reading. • Create study guides for review.			
5. Using memory tools • Get adequate sleep. • Review immediately. • Study regularly. • Organize/categorize. • Use my senses. • Associate.			

6. Preparing well for tests
• Stay current with work.
• Make review guides.
• Rehearse.
• Manage worry and anxiety.
• Practice reading and answering test items:
  • True/False
  • Multiple Choice
  • Essay			

Conclusion

Critical
Thinking
Task

The following checklist of items was presented in the Conclusion of Chapter 1. Review the checklist, and determine to how many of the items you can confidently answer yes. Use the checklist periodically to keep yourself on the track to academic success.

- ○ 1. Are you clear about why you are attending college and what you expect to get out of college?
- ○ 2. Do you know what each instructor expects of you? Have you read—and reread—each syllabus and met with the instructor? Have you regularly attended review sessions?
- ○ 3. Are you managing your time wisely? Are you assessing your priorities periodically and establishing a routine that balances your academic, personal, and social/leisure demands?
- ○ 4. Are you using effective methods of study for each course?
- ○ 5. Are you involving yourself in college life by participating in campus activities?
- ○ 6. Are you avoiding these hazards?
  - Mishandling of your personal freedom and time.
  - Misuse of alcohol and drugs.
  - Mishandling of your personal health.
  - Mishandling of your best interests.

As you monitor and adjust how you study and learn, note the sense of self-confidence and empowerment that accompanies your development as a student and a learner. The skills, attitudes, and self-knowledge that lead you toward success in college also will serve you well out of college as you fulfill your career aspirations and personal goals.

REFERENCES

Briggs, K. C., & Myers, I. B. (1998). *Myers-Briggs Type Indicator*, Form M. Palo Alto, CA: Consulting Psychologists Press. *Myers-Briggs Type Indicator* and MBTI are registered trademarks of Consulting Psychologists Press, Inc., Palo Alto, CA.

Weinstein, C.E., & Palmer, D. R. (2002). *Learning and study strategies inventory* (2nd ed.). Clearwater, FL: H & H Publishing.

INDEX